HOMETOWN

HOME

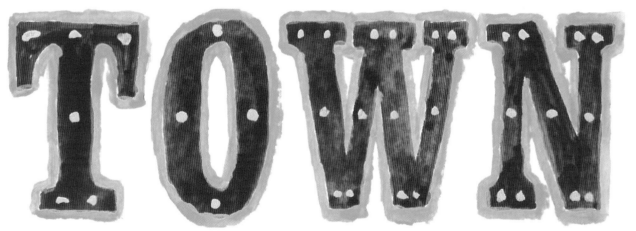

TOWN

OUT AND ABOUT IN VICTORIA'S NEIGHBOURHOODS

Written by
ANNY SCOONES

Illustrated by
ROBERT AMOS

TouchWood
Editions

TouchWood Editions
touchwoodeditions.com

LIBRARY AND ARCHIVES CANADA CATALOGUING IN PUBLICATION
Scoones, Anny, 1957–
Hometown : out and about in Victoria's neighbourhoods
/ Anny Scoones ; Robert Amos, illustrator.

Also issued in electronic format.
ISBN 978-1-77151-000-4

1. Victoria (BC)—Description and travel. 2. Victoria
(BC)—Pictorial works. I. Amos, Robert, 1950– II. Title.

FC3846.18.S36 2013   917.11'28045   C2012-907748-8

Editor: Marlyn Horsdal
Proofreader: Vivian Sinclair
Design: Pete Kohut
Cover and interior illustrations: Robert Amos, except pages 23, 52,
128, 129, and 154, which have illustrations by Sarah Amos

We gratefully acknowledge the financial support for our publishing activities from the Government of Canada through the Canada Book Fund, Canada Council for the Arts, and the province of British Columbia through the British Columbia Arts Council and the Book Publishing Tax Credit.

This book was produced using FSC®-certified, acid-free paper, processed chlorine free and printed with soya-based inks.

2   3   4   5   17   16   15   14   13

This book is dedicated to Victoria's many volunteers, stewards, "friends," and societies who devote many hours of personal care to keep our neighbourhoods clean, safe, and beautiful. To all of you who clean our streams, make soup, pull invasive ivy, plan for neighbourhood emergencies, preserve our historic cemeteries, beautify Ogden Point, prune the roses and tend the alpine rockery at Government House, create public compost, restore turtle habitat, and serve our community in many other countless ways because you care, this book is for you with gratitude and admiration.

And to my new friends at the Victoria International Academy.

From Beacon Hill

CONTENTS

The Parliament Buildings

Introduction

This book celebrates Victoria's neighbourhoods and surrounding region. It is not a book of facts, but rather a gentle stroll through our region during which we pause, observe, ponder, and have what I like to call "a little think" on the various features and personalities of these areas and how these features not only create a neighbourhood, and therefore our city, but also how they make us *feel*, how they "move" us.

Our little thinks can include marvelling at the charming, hard-working winter wren who builds a vast array of tiny reed-and-grass houses hoping to attract a female, or experiencing the rowdy fun of "Uke Night," when fifty people get together to play their ukuleles, or wondering why certain public art makes us stop and gaze in awe, or asking which is lovelier, a man-made environment or a natural one. These and many other features are explored here as we amble through our city.

As we consider our neighbourhoods' diverse personalities, we will see the many subtle elements that bind us all together—things such as the poems by our Poet Laureate, Janet Rogers (two of which are in this book); the thousand-plus hanging flower baskets that line our downtown streets; the Netherlands carillon that fills the Inner Harbour with joyful music on a bleak and dismal winter's day; and the corner stores, always there, with their overflowing buckets of colourful bouquets under their awnings.

I hope the observations and thoughts in this book, along with Robert's lovely paintings, bring you many little thinks and much joy about Victoria and our place within it.

Tripping Through Paradise
Janet Rogers

we take
earthquake rides
over rock waves
kissing
lake faces
stretching past
grass lands
and heifer spotted
landscapes

road signs
promise
moose-elk-deer
eyes peeled for
big footed men
and our reflections
in stone
emotional
ups and downs
crowned at
toothy summits
sliver wide highways
balanced between

judgment and progress

referendum deals

gone dead
stirred up
deep beds
laid to rest
new relationships
of silence
and inertia

these lands
grow and recede
and always
teach
us ways
to get around
shows us where
the trails lead

to live
in this land
you must understand
real histories
still lived

"No, that's not
a ski slope
that's a mountain
we pray there."

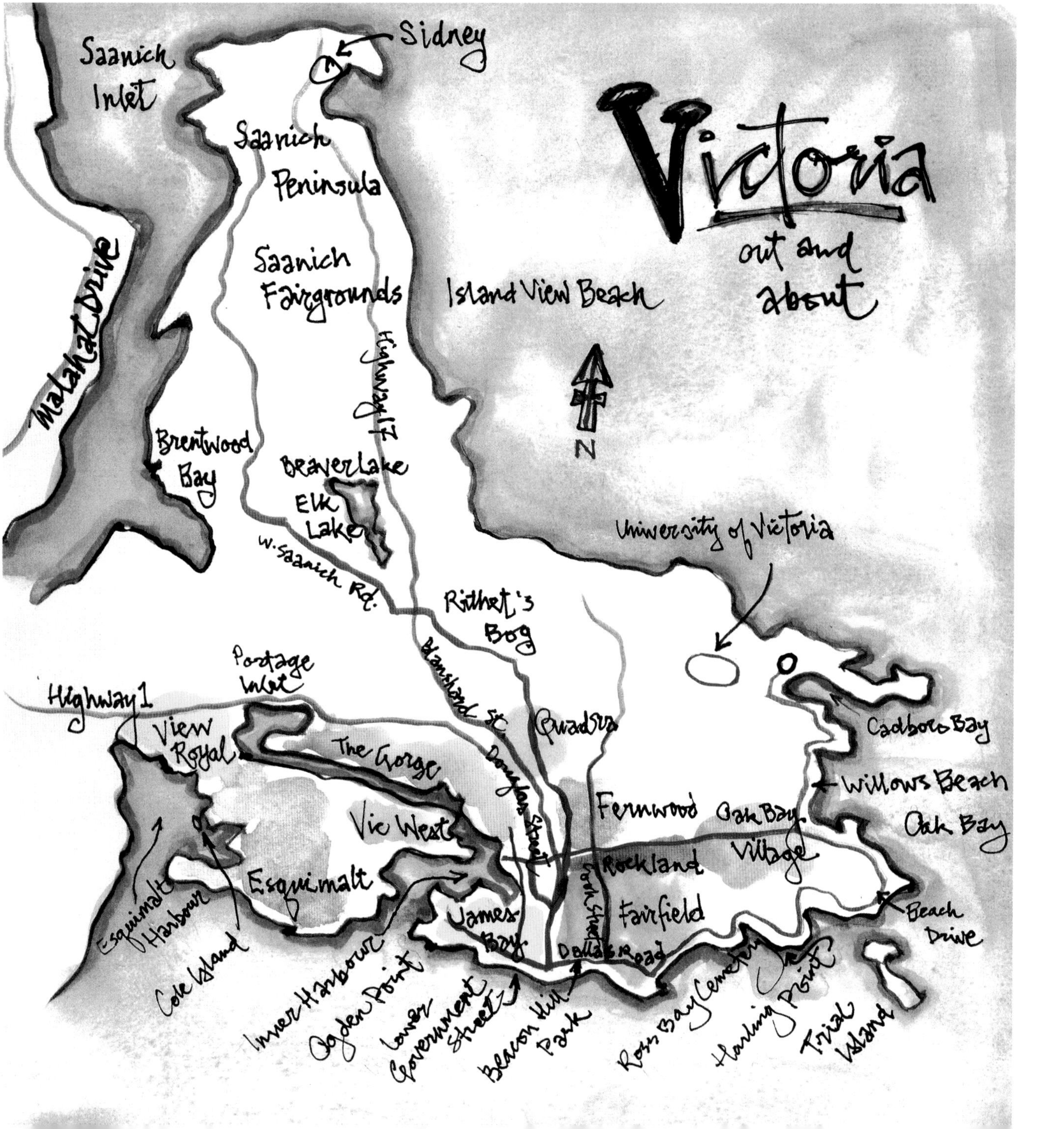

Sidney

Saanich
Inlet

Saanich
Peninsula

Saanich
Fairgrounds

Island View Beach

Victoria
out and about

Matahat Drive

Brentwood
Bay

Beaver Lake
Elk
Lake

Highway 17

N

University of Victoria

W. Saanich Rd.

Rithet's
Bog

Portage
Inlet

Highway 1

View
Royal

The Gorge

Blanshard St.

Quadra

Cadboro Bay

Willows Beach

Oak Bay

Vic West

Douglas Street

Fernwood

Oak Bay
Village

Esquimalt
Harbour

Esquimalt

Rockland

Fairfield

Cole Island

Inner Harbour

Ogden Point

Lower
Government
Street

James
Bay

Cook Street

Dallas Road

Beacon Hill
Park

Ross Bay Cemetery

Harling Point

Beach
Drive

Trial Island

Anny's House

CHAPTER ONE

James Bay

I moved into a solid little white house with red trim and leaded-glass windows, a back garden and two apple trees, a fragrant old jasmine leaning against a small weathered garage and a wild array of spindly, yellow and purple snapdragons. It was built in 1911. Around the corner, in a sooty brownstone building with a green door, was a woman selling her homemade meat pies. One of my first impressions of James Bay, therefore, was that the residents here had a sense of how to take care of themselves and each other, and I was to discover more of this on my walks through this eclectic old neighbourhood. There's a man who plants rows and rows of lush kale, lettuce, spinach, and other vegetables in his front garden, free for the taking, and the less fortunate and the eccentrics, some who talk to themselves as they ride around on colourful scooters covered with decals and dangling knick-knacks, seem to be subtly under the locals' caring and watchful eyes—the owner of the flower shop, the three men who share a cigar on the corner bench every morning, the woman who feeds the birds on the boulevards.

At Christmas, a man selling wreaths made from native plants stood in the rain in front of an unwashed tile mosaic of a mermaid at James Bay Square. Dripping and cold, he explained that he was out of work but had created the lovely wreaths of leafy green salal, with the white touches of snowberry and auburn of wild crabapple.

Alice Mary, my portly old black Labrador, could not get up the steps of the house, so she had to succumb to living in the basement, which was at ground level—she had a grand bed down there, blankets and old feather duvets piled on the grey concrete floor next to the huge, shiny oil tank. She was very comfortable amongst the boxes of my childhood photographs—photographs of me playing in the huge snowbanks in Fredericton, grinning a toothless grin at six years old, in my blue snowsuit and thick red scarf, crawling through a snow tunnel. Another box contained my thirty dirty troll dolls and horse tack now rarely used. Saanich Fair displays, neatly packed in blue rubber totes, that I had used every year to decorate the pig stalls were stacked against the cool stone foundation—great red and purple swaths of cloth and gold silk flowers, as well as posters and information sheets about Mabel and Matilda, the two huge Gloucester Old Spot sows (whom I left back on Glamorgan Farm in North Saanich).

Alice Mary loves to be in the basement. She only has to lumber up one little cement step to the back lawn, where she peacefully dozes under the apple trees beside the big blue ceramic pot (which I lugged from the farm) full to overflowing with yellow and cherry-red petunias. On warm summer days, Alice sniffs the fresh sea breeze wafting up our quiet street from nearby Dallas Road. Just before the great move to James Bay took place, I called our dear veterinarian to the farm to put Alice Mary down—she

is after all seventeen! And she had been having intestinal troubles which I will not go into—suffice to say it wasn't a pretty sight, and my wool rugs were becoming stained and ruined.

The nice veterinarian came to the farm and looked at Alice Mary, who was restless and panting under the grand old honeysuckle bush, and said that she'd be back later to do the deed, and would I like to bury her on the farm or have her cremated? I thought she should rest in peace with all the other dear creatures who were on the farm—lots of Naked Neck chickens, the old pony Napoleon and his scrawny, sad pal Kyle (an ex-racehorse), Buster, the most affectionate pig I have ever met, and Norman, the stray cat who crawled into the house one wet howling night and stayed for years. The vet gave Alice a pill to make her comfortable and left, and I went about my chores. Suddenly I heard a gastric commotion from Alice Mary's rear end on the lawn. On close inspection, I found two excreted slimy Brillo pads, probably from the barbecue. Alice Mary has been fine ever since that day of the great excretion and has made it to James Bay.

There is also a furnace in the basement of our new house. A great big old tin box whose filters I have been instructed to change regularly—I don't have a clue what that means. But I couldn't believe it the first morning when I woke up (during a very cold, late, damp spring)

Glamorgan Farm

and only had to touch a blinking green switch to feel a surge of soft hot air (they call it forced air) surrounding me as I had my coffee in the front room and studied the wooden heritage houses with their ornate verandas and hanging baskets across the street. (One must keep a clean house if one has forced air, because there I was, warm, but surrounded by blowing, swirling dust and a lot of pet hair.) It is then, in the white morning, when the salty chill has settled down Medana Street, with the warm heat inside, that I have my first little thinks of the day.

On the farm I had to venture out across a cold, wet meadow in a raw, dark-blue dawn in my nightie, rubber boots, and wet work gloves to a wood pile, load my arms full of heavy, knotty logs and spend an hour lighting the fire. There was no time to have a little think because then I had to feed the pigs— they would wake up and want their warm slop when they saw my porch light go on—and then the

chickens would be awakened by the grunting of the pigs, and then the horses would come to life because of the cackling in the coop, and before long it would be lunchtime and I still hadn't had my cherished little think, so I'd have it when I cleaned their pens later in the day. This is why I quite like my furnace and forced air.

The uninsulated attic reminded me of the great barn on the farm—the smell of red-cedar beams made it a perfect place to write, I thought. But the narrow staircase was too small to take furniture up, so I bought simple pine chairs that one puts together with little screws and bolts. I assembled everything as the barn cats, whom I had brought from the farm, looked on from the nooks and crannies between the beams; they thought they had moved into another barn, but this one was warmer, and they thought the chairs with their lovely red cushions looked quite cozy.

In the small back garden I had two raised beds built by a dear man from down the street—he built the beds and filled them with soil in one day! I was amazed at his energy (he also insulated the basement) until he told me that he was bipolar, and we had a little joke that he must have been on a high to have worked so fast. I promised him vegetables in the summer, and when summer came I gave him, among other things, a lovely big round purple cabbage, which he loved; he said that purple cabbage helps bipolar people—it helps their nerves. I made

salad bouquets from mustard greens, arugula, French sorrel, kale, baby broccoli sprouts, beet tops, parsley, green onions, and edible flowers.

Our street is lined with pink-blossomed hawthorn trees—some people call them may trees. Gran always said that you should never bring hawthorn into the house, that it would bring bad luck. Other streets are lined with flowering plums or cherries, or chestnut or beech trees. Residents plant bulbs randomly on the boulevards—the city doesn't mind at all! So this autumn I planted some daffodils around the hawthorn tree, plus a few red tulips here and there, and in the spring the man on the ride-on mower neatly mowed around each one. That meant something to me, the fact that he just didn't mow them all down—I should write to the City and tell them how I appreciate the care that their workers take.

It amazed me that on one of my first days in my dear little house, as I was sitting looking out the front window, a girl drove up and from a hose attached to a water tank on the back of her small truck, she watered a newly planted young hawthorn. It filled me with joy and hope for the world that a human being would actually come around and water the street trees, much as a lamplighter used to come around and light the street lamps at dusk. I hope there will always be a job for a human to do publicly on a regular schedule—it seems to give us a special type of certainty and security just to know that the streets and trees are being cared for, that the city has an ordered routine. It's as if we are all being taken care of; human labour connects us to a feeling of home and comfort when we see people physically, looking after our community.

A few minutes after the tree-watering girl left, there was a solid and steady clip-clop echoing on the street, and a great grey horse strolled passed the window, pulling a white carriage carrying a happy-looking family, as the driver, a girl in black wearing a little top hat, described some local history. "This area used to be Beckley Farm," I heard her say as she gently held the leather reins and the grey's head bobbed with every step. "Some of these houses are brightly coloured and that's a sign of wealth!" she said, and I looked at my dear little peeling white house with affection.

I love the horses—they line up near the Parliament Buildings at the Inner Harbour every morning for their day's work. They are tied under great shady trees and have bowls of oats and alfalfa cubes, and huge rubber buckets of water. They never complain, these gentle giants, and plod along faithfully, giving the tourists a good look at this quirky and historic neighbourhood. On Canada Day the horses wear red hats and Canadian flags that are tucked onto their thick plaited forelocks, and at Christmas they wear holly sprigs and little brass bells hung from their harnesses. The girls who drive the horses wear top hats, pink lipstick, and dark green silk cummerbunds. They keep the streets hosed and braid the horses' tails in elegant French braids, sometimes entwining the braids with flowers and plumes. On damp, misty mornings we can smell the subtle odour of manure and mare's urine mixed with the sea drifting up the foggy streets.

The history of a city is a funny thing—the same features exist now as long ago, such as the horses, but the purposes have changed; horses used to be a form of transportation, and now their purpose is tourism. I think it's a fine sign of a tasteful and sophisticated city when it can adapt a historical feature in a modern way; Victoria is brilliant at this, adapting to modernism using the best of its history, and we can see this in all of the neighbourhoods. Victoria respects, and has not forgotten,

Canadian Coast Guard Station, Odgen Point

its roots, and has established its identity from its colourful history.

The horses load and unload in the works yard at nearby Ogden Point, near the cruise-ship terminal. It's rather an austere and empty space, a quiet area between the blue-and-white Harbour Authority offices and a seaside café. Here is where the horses can rest and eat their hay surrounded by the city's marine-infrastructure equipment: stacks of creosoted planks, stockpiles of rusted marine paraphernalia, boat propellers, engines, ropes, and weathered vessels on blocks about to topple over.

The enormous white cruise ships dock just yards away, as well as the yellow Search and Rescue dinghies, solid little tugs with chimneys, and the occasional foreign visiting vessel, all tied to the massive steel girders on the protruding wharves.

For about a week one summer, the elegant Chilean naval-training ship *Esmeralda* was tied to the Ogden Point dock. I could see it from the beaches on Dallas Road, and every morning as Archie, my new hound companion, and I climbed over the damp black rocks of the shore, we could hear the lively brass band on the ship playing a morning tune through the dawn mist as they raised both the Chilean and the Canadian flags. I cannot really explain why, but this daily dawn tradition of the brass band and the flag raising was quite moving—the little musical tradition was dwarfed by the immense, green, turbulent sea and snowcapped mountains. They acknowledged their Canadian port and their naval tasks before they quietly raised their billowing white sails to continue on their travels.

Part of the fun of moving into a new neighbourhood is exploring its cultural features. For entertainment in James Bay, I noticed that the White Eagle Polish Hall, a rectangular white-stucco building up by the baseball diamond, tennis courts, and communal garden plots, was having a traditional Polish lunch for ten dollars, and farther along the street, near where the Coast Guard stores its red-enamel buoys, chains, and great piles of ropes, there was to be a Big Band evening at the Edelweiss Club, a fundraiser for the hard of hearing.

It seems somebody once made a serious effort to bring public art to James Bay. It's a funny thing about public art—sometimes when a deliberate attempt is made to enrich culture, the art is simply ignored, deteriorates, or is even vandalized, and other times, when public art is created spontaneously, it is treasured and becomes an intricate (and intimate) part of the personality of the neighbourhood. At one time, James Bay was beautified by adding tile mosaics in various locations in the village, and today they look a little tired, but the tired look actually suits the neighbourhood. On the other hand, there are graffiti and murals

Ogden Point

The Ogden Point breakwater was constructed from millions of tons of cement and granite slabs in the early 1900s in anticipation of increased sea trade from the construction of the Panama Canal. The unmanned lighthouse with an electric foghorn was added in 1919.

It is worth a stroll to the end of the breakwater just to get a sense of the scale of the project and to see the granite slabs. One of the most amazing things, given that we are in an age of fear of liability, is that there is no guard rail—you are out there in the fresh sea breeze with the great jade-grey waves crashing below your feet. It's a wild ocean walk on a stormy day!

The waters around the breakwater are a popular diving area. Today, Ogden Point is used mainly as a docking spot for numerous cruise ships, usually heading up to Alaska, and other visiting and Coast Guard vessels.

The Ogden Point breakwater and docking area are under the watchful eye of the Ogden Point Enhancement Society (established in 1996). The society has contributed to beautifying the area as a lovely public space with informative kiosks, benches, pocket gardens, walkways, and viewpoints, which make it very attractive to the ships' tourists as well as to the locals.

One of the most impressive features of Ogden Point is the Unity Wall, also known as "the land and sea mural." The Unity Wall is the world's longest mural and is on one side of the breakwater. The mural depicts the rich spiritual and traditional cultures, symbolism, legends, teachings, and history of the Salish Nations and was created by local First Nations students.

Emily Carr's Birthplace

that are glowing with life and were completely unplanned. Sometimes we just cannot plan or dictate "beauty"—a neighbourhood has to take its own form.

Just up the street from my house is Emily Carr's house, her birthplace, and now a museum, a lovely yellow Victorian house with primroses and little pink tea roses in a circular garden in the front. Gravel pathways wind their way between lilies and fragrant mock orange shrubs and lilacs. I wonder if Emily Carr even had tea. She was so rustic—or at least she became that way. I can picture her sitting on a tree stump in the woods that she loved, surrounded by her beloved grey salt- and wind-weathered leaning totem poles, drinking strong, day-old coffee from a rusted and chipped enameled pot; I can't really see her drinking tea in her forest days. Just because she lived (at one time) in an elegant town in an English society and did lovely watercolours (one of my favourites is of Beacon Hill Park, looking up the hill) doesn't really mean she "took" tea from little china cups, does it? Well, maybe it does. Her fingers became so thick and muscular, I doubt she could even fit her finger through the delicate handle of a teacup. Maybe she had some kind of First Nations tea made from roots or berries.

My grandfather, Harold Mortimer-Lamb, Mum's father, also lived here in James Bay. He did photography in his spare time and was a friend of Emily's. (Mum says he invented a way of taking photographs at night. "But in the daytime," she says with a laugh, "I remember him taking photos under a blanket.") In fact, Grandpa Harold took a photograph of Emily Carr, the one with her arms crossed, wearing a little cap, hard and weathered, staring at the camera. I have the photo, and I also have an ashtray she made with local clay; it looks like a whale's mouth, and it's painted with First Nations symbols in red and dark green and signed on the bottom right in the clay: Klee Wyck. I suppose she gave it to my grandfather—they were both in the local art world—although Mum says they had a big disagreement. Emily actually hit Harold (in the days long before the word "abuse" was used). That was the end of the relationship; she was hot-tempered and made art, and he was cold and aloof and collected art—small wonder that they parted, but completely understandable that they met and conversed, for a while at least.

People are very friendly in James Bay. The other day a nice man who collects buckets of household compost on the back of his bicycle stopped to rest, and we chatted (I was planting cauliflower in the front garden). Somehow we got talking about plastics. He told me that there is an amoeba in the Amazon that eats plastic—LOVES plastic—but that it is contained. Imagine if the amoeba got loose! Wouldn't it be ironic if the world ended because of a plastic-eating creature? It would eat your car bumpers and most of the contents in a Hawaiian gift shop, and then consume your credit cards for dessert—it would be the demise of Western civilization!

Here is something else about James Bay: if people don't want something, they put it on the street for the taking. This habit was absolutely outlawed by Victoria's first mayor, Thomas Harris, in 1862. The first time I saw this interesting tradition was the day after I moved in. Archie was dragging me down the street because he saw a little dog in the distance (it's a strange dog—he has no hair, but his skin is a lovely deep chestnut-brown, and he is walked by a little Spanish man). A lady came out of a pink house and put a box of old cassette tapes under a tree with a sign saying PLEASE HELP YOURSELF. The next day her neighbour put out a futon (with limited stains) and an electric toothbrush (*with* the brush). Her sign simply said TAKE AWAY—and someone did!

I had done some sorting for the move and was also having some electrical work done in our dear little white house, so I decided to try this method of disposal. I went out at dawn and on the boulevard I gingerly set out a book on menopause, a dirty, yellowed plastic chandelier with half its "drops" missing, some broken smoke alarms, my battered riding helmet, and a pair of yoga leotards. My feeble little note in black marker said

FREE FOR YOU TODAY! NO HST. I was nervous that nobody would want my goods, but everything was gone by noon! One day, a few blocks away, I spied a huge, rather mildewed book of *New Yorker* cartoons, which I grabbed (on top of a blue velour recliner with a missing lever).

The book amused me all afternoon as I sat with Alice Mary and Archie on the back lawn amongst my pink-tinged cauliflower (due to being planted beside the beets) and my cabbages, which were becoming so large that they were splitting. There was a wonderful cartoon of a dog in a business suit, carrying a briefcase, leaning over a bar, and the bartender (who was a man) said, "The usual? Scotch and toilet water?" And another of two men walking their dogs in the park, and one dog was tiny, *really* tiny, and the man walking this tiny dog said, "Yes, they used to be bred as hors d'oeuvres." Well, when I finished the book I put it back out on the boulevard, and it quickly disappeared.

One day I picked up a candle holder—a curly, black, ornate thing with dirty glass cups that held little candles, but as soon as I got it into the kitchen to clean it, I regretted picking it up. Why did I? Because it was free and I like candles, and because it was there in front of me at that moment, and I grabbed it without thinking. Gosh, I can understand why some people become hoarders. Late that night, when I took Archie around the block for his nightly walk, I discreetly put the candle holder back on the boulevard whence it came, and it was gone at dawn.

Every morning and late afternoon, I walk Archie to the beaches along Dallas Road. Archie went to dog school, but it didn't do a thing for him. He pulls me down the street in his new red harness; one of my arms is stretched beyond belief from holding him, the other arm flails sideways, waving the little blue disposal bag. He can hardly wait to get to the beach, a place where I feel the closest to heaven, so I can hardly wait to get there too!

Along the way we pass all sorts of houses painted in shades of teal, purple, and burgundy—that's something special I love about James Bay. All the homes and yards and gardens are so varied, no one garden or front yard is like another—there is no pressure to conform. There's an old stone house with a lime-green picket fence and a purple house with turrets covered in climbing honeysuckle that stretches up to a little balcony where, at night, a thin man with a wispy beard strums on a guitar.

Many houses in James Bay are from the late 1800s and early 1900s. In the Victorian era, homes were painted in bright colours—usually three, including the trim—in order to accentuate the elegant decorative designs around the windows, balconies, doors, and eaves. These colourful homes were called "painted ladies."

There's a little cottage with moss on the roof, barely visible behind a mass of quince, lilac, and clematis gone wild. There's a house that puts dog water out in an old saucepan under some hanging baskets of geraniums. A rare sight is a red-brick house. There is one on our walk, covered in pale yellow climbing roses that lead up to a white railing piled with an endless array of clay flower pots. There is a large, elegant, dark green-shingled house with a wraparound veranda, and in the window is an enormous sculpture of a voluptuous, curvy, copper scallop shell. And there's one house with numerous hanging baskets dangling from its porch, but on closer inspection they are not baskets at all; they are bicycle helmets full of little succulents and sedums.

That's the thing about James Bay: everyone can be unique without feeling odd—everything

is accepted. I don't think anything would shock James Bay. It's had a rough history but remains quite unjaded. Besides being an original farm that grew food for the workers who were busy building the city, the far end of James Bay—which is now the cruise-ship port and home of the city's Coast Guard docks, backed by glimmering turquoise glass penthouses—was a shipyard, historically considered a seedy and dangerous place for young girls to go. I met a woman named Frances at the Stroke Recovery Club (I haven't had a stroke—I go there to read to them) and she told me that she lived in James Bay as a girl but was never allowed to go below Oswego Street or her father would take the belt to her. So James Bay has had this rather sordid, boisterous past, not the quaint tea party, ice cream parlour and toffee-shoppe past found in other neighbourhoods, but its history has perhaps given it its wonderful variety and the tolerance I feel when I walk the streets.

I passed a little house one day with a mass of wildflowers covering the front garden—poppies and goldenrod and marigold mixed with grass and shrubs, all slowly going back to nature, contained by a rotting fence and shaded by a great leafy maple. Pinned to the fence was a poem, the paper slightly mildewed, and beside the poem was a photograph of a scruffy bearded man in a soiled red coat. He was a local character, homeless, who had died, and someone had written this poem to honour him, to offer him a little dignity—that's James Bay. Some red plastic flowers had been placed in the fence, just beneath his photo.

You can smell the damp sea air and hear the cries of seagulls all through the day. People find seagulls (and crows) bothersome, but I think they are very intelligent and, more important, compassionate—they take care of each other. There was a sad little seagull in our neighbourhood when we moved here. He was a feeble, thin, grey bird who spent his days crying on top of our roof. The neighbours and I soon deduced that he couldn't fly. In fact, one day he tumbled off the roof and landed in my kale, and Archie went hysterical! Somehow, the bird managed to crawl and hop onto the garage roof, which is flat, where he remained for days while numerous other seagulls called to him and brought him mouthfuls of food, which looked to be mostly shellfish and seaweed (the shells are still on the roof). His family never disowned him, but stayed by him until he could fly away, which he eventually did about three weeks later, and the neighbours and I all watched and rooted for the little fellow as he flapped off toward the beach, surrounded by his relations.

Two crows have built a big nest of sticks in the hawthorn tree outside my office window. One day I saw a robin flying desperately at them above the power lines—the bad crows had stolen the robin's eggs, and she was in despair. Oh, nature can be so cruel, sometimes more cruel than we can be—we have the power to be kind. Mum told me a horrific story of seeing two crows go after a young eagle that had raided their nest; they swarmed the eagle like a pair of bullies and forced him down into the river, where they drowned the poor screaming bird. On the other hand, Mum also tells the story of two crows that live in her garden and have babies every year; one year they had a little white crow! They protected it fiercely and it never left home; all three still reside in Mum's apple tree, years later.

Finally Archie and I arrive at the Dallas Road seafront, the place where we heard the brass band from the Chilean ship in the mist. In the meadow above the seafront is a man-made pond where elderly men periodically reenact the Battle of the North Atlantic with their remote-controlled miniature war vessels.

Like many other road names and landmarks in Victoria, Dallas Road is named after an officer of the Hudson's Bay Company. A.G. Dallas was also a son-in-law of James Douglas. Dallas Road stretches along the whitecapped, bottle-green sea. On windy days the sea pounds against the black lava and rose-pink granite shore, which is heavily scratched from past glacier action and pocketed with little living tidal pools with busy creatures darting about their day's duties.

At one end (the cruise-ship end) of the walkway is a solid cement barricade, pockmarked and painted light aqua. It looks as if it is from another era and place—perhaps from a British seaside town where you might see a man selling little ice creams and popsicles from a musical cart, and red-striped deck chairs on the promenade, and peppermint sticks being sold from a beach kiosk. I love this

barricade, but I have a rather sad feeling that it will be replaced one day by something slick and new. What a shame that will be—another tradition to say goodbye to. I am sure some people think that the heavy old sea-sprayed "wall" is ugly. It's *not* pretty, but it's *better* than pretty. There's even an old concrete gunnery halfway along, which leads down to the sandy beach, the bottom few steps covered in green seaweed and barnacles. I met an old man one day who was strolling the sand at low tide, and he told me that he remembers the gunnery also being used as a lifeguard station.

I worry sometimes that we are too "pretty" oriented—I wonder why everything always has to be pretty and hope that sometimes character and ambience can be considered as valuable as prettiness. That's why I love Bob McDonald, the man on the CBC who does the science programs—he never straightened his teeth!

Archie and I wade through the waist-high grass toward the cement steps to the beach. In summer the grasses quiver in the breeze and reveal a meadow of mauves and jades, making room for the delicate wild onion and white yarrow. Great shrubberies of Nootka rose, hawthorns and poplars huddle together in thick, dense clusters to break the winter sea gales that come roaring up the cliffs.

Under an old, lone, worn and ragged crabapple tree, covered in a tangle of sticks and thick vegetation, is a weatherworn granite stone, engraved to the memory of a five-year-old girl named Bertha who arrived on a ship from San Francisco in 1872. The little girl had smallpox and was placed in a pest house (on Dallas Road), where she died. The title "pest house" sounds dirty, even rather naughty, as if it were a place of debauchery, but it actually was like a sanatorium where people were quarantined if they had one of the dreaded diseases of the time, such as cholera, tuberculosis, or smallpox. Sadly, pest houses usually included graveyards.

Archie and I pass the stone for little Bertha, so I think about her every day, and I am moved that the City Parks workers, big, burly men in orange rubber overalls, cut the grasses back just a little, so that her stone receives a sliver of sunlight but not too much attention, on their twice-a-year mowings; it's as if they too respect her short little life, which ended very near this grassy wild spot. Her stone overlooks the sea from under the black branches dotted with small, round orange fruit; saturated by the rains, the crabapples drop around her as food for the winter birds.

We've come far with science and health and disease since Bertha died in the Dallas Road pest house, but in other ways we seem to have *new* health troubles—I wonder if we'll ever get it right. Perhaps our vast knowledge of medicine today is a curse—now that we know so many cures, we can relax a little and therefore allow other ailments to creep in. We seem to be so confident of our good life that it has taken the edge off prevention, as if we are verging on overindulgence.

A short stroll past Bertha's stone is a monument honouring Marilyn Bell, who braved our cold green waters in 1956 and swam the strait, the first woman to do so; she was also the first to swim across Lake Ontario and the youngest to swim the English Channel. Her stone, amongst the spring

bluebells on Dallas Road, is more visible, bigger, and a little fancier than Bertha's, with an etched picture of her head, smiling and wearing a bathing cap.

In the spring, the meadows along Dallas Road are a sea of bluebells, followed two weeks later by a rush of deep cobalt camas. The banks are a mass of wild, pale yellow lupines, so delicate in appearance yet so strong, the way they hang on to the sandy banks during the winter storms; they grow amongst a tangle of magenta sweet peas. Clusters of sea-battered, thorny yellow gorse lean stiffly toward the street from years of bowing against the wind and salt, and below, between the black rocks and pink granite of the shoreline are sea-washed beaches of pebbles, shells, and sea glass. Whenever I see sea glass, those little jewel-like, salt-washed pieces of glass amongst the sand and shells, I think

of Mother Nature reclaiming what is hers—sand.

The oystercatchers and great blue herons are on the rocks every morning as the tides change, picking in the hidden crevices and the thick kelp beds for a meal, and in late autumn the dear little harlequin ducks appear, distinguished by their auburn sides and striking white markings, bobbing and diving in the waves between the black rocks. They winter on the coast and return inland to breed in the spring, the only sea ducks that need inland whitewater streams as part of their life cycle; there they lay their eggs on the streambanks, hidden in hollowed trees and in the thick, sheltered underbrush. Their feather designs are so magnificent that they are also known as the "circus duck." They make a little peep-peep squeak, which I can hear on the beach, and it is because of this sound that they are also called the "sea mouse."

Archie and I climb over the rocks and logs for miles—that way we can visit the little hidden bays and take in more of the sea. There are fewer people down below—often only signs that people have been there. Somebody at night on occasion crochets a red woollen spiderweb between the washed-in logs! I often sit on a bleached log or on the great black rocks and have a little think while Archie sniffs and paddles or chews on a stick.

The beauty of the sea and shore has me in awe every time I stop and feel it. One of the most magical parts of our walks along the shore are the tidal pools—little communities full of shimmering blue and silver shells, delicate, pearl-white sea anemones swaying in the cool water amongst seaweeds of amber and burgundy, and the tiny busy sea life scurrying to and fro, trying to get their chores finished on their tight timeline. That is when the tide returns with its surging mighty force that covers the rocks until it retreats again, right on Mother Nature's schedule—Mother Nature has an amazing datebook! Her monthly planner is far more accurate than ours, and she rarely misses an appointment.

When the tide is high, the emerald eelgrass holds tight, the little creatures go into their homes (their shells), gripping the rock with every ounce of their strength, and all is asleep and calm inside. But sometimes, in the wild winter storms, a huge, thick mound of kelp can wash onto the shore, and within it are strange creatures that have been unable to stay in the sea due to the force of the waves—red-shelled creatures with soft blanched underbellies are tossed onto the shore, chitons that have been ripped from their rocks— Mother Nature is amazing, but she can be cruel.

One day I looked at a tidal pool when the sun made it glitter even more. It was truly one of the most beautiful sights I have ever seen; well, let's say *felt*. There's a difference, I think, between what we see and what we feel (sometimes I wonder what moves me more, what I see or what I feel). So this little tidal pool, shimmering in the sun like a jewel box, was so beautiful, full of garnets and opals, but it also moved me because it was full of activity, just what nature intended. All the busy creatures were moving around finding dinner and cleaning the little pool and preparing for the high tide and not needing any praise or attention for just living the life that Mother Nature gave them. And then I saw the bobbing cigarette butt. The cigarette butt "rained on my parade."

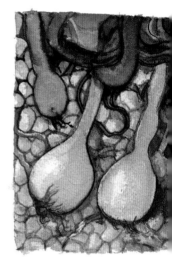

I felt so sorry for the little tidal pool. I scooped the butt out and put it in one of Archie's dog-litter bags. And then I had this thought, a reaction, of apologizing to the tidal pool, to the beach, to the sea. If I were a poet, I would write a poem called "Apology to the Beach." The final lines would be:

I'm so sorry, beach,
Sorry to the sea,
Something something something,
(about interfering with Mother Nature)
For man's careless indignity.

Or something like that. I might have a line about how the sea would forgive us, would adjust or just carry on. I am not sure how to write a poem, but I wish I knew—just to capture the rise of the heart at particular moments.

(The other poem I always wanted to write was about the complete in-aweness—I made up that word, but I think in poetry one is allowed—and pleasure I had when eating a pork roast with the warm crackling—the fat was so delicious, all over my lips, running down my chin. I was sucking on it and I remember thinking, "This is so good that I can't tell where my lips end and the crackling begins," and then I saw that the crackling also had some hair on it, cooked, of course, and I thought, "This is the only time in my life when I will eat hair and moan about how delicious it is." That would be some poem! The moment of bliss with fat and hair, the absolute pleasure, sitting there in my drafty blue kitchen in the old log farmhouse on Glamorgan Farm, the air thick with steam and woodsmoke, eating that warm, thick, fat crackling!)

These are the types of little thinks I have while staring into the lovely tidal pools on the beach in James Bay. James Bay encourages, and makes possible, these little thinks.

After I saw that cigarette butt, I noticed other things—plastic bags and bits of rope and some unmentionables. At first I used a stick to pick up things that I didn't want to touch, but then I bought some blue rubber gloves. I began to pick up these foreign objects and lug them up to the freshly painted dark green litter baskets that sit in the grassy meadows above.

My friend Lorna says that I have simply transferred from picking up manure all day on the farm to picking up trash in town. But at least I may be saving a life by picking up plastic bags—sea mammals think that plastic bags are jellyfish and swallow them, with dire consequences. I'd like to tell you of one more incident on the beach.

One day Archie was climbing all over the rocks and I, with my keen eye, was picking up bits of litter—candy wrappers, bottle caps, and such. I usually leave the returnable beer cans and wine bottles for others to pick up, but on this particular day, I put a beer can in my bag. I had stupidly put Archie's new red leash down someplace and couldn't find it, so I used an old rope I'd found to lead him back up to the meadow to dispose of our day's loot. It was incredibly windy, so I know I looked dishevelled, and I was wearing my grubby barn clothes as I planned to go and see my horse after Archie's walk. So I was quite windswept, with a torn bag full of garbage with a beer can on top and a dog on a frayed rope pulling me up the steps. Halfway up, under a thick canopy of shady overgrowth, stood a slim, tanned, older woman in a large straw hat, a form-fitting lime-green shirt, white jeans and sandals, with some gold chains around her neck. She handed me a ten-dollar bill and said she hoped it would buy me a good meal! And then she gave me another five-dollar bill for "food for your dog!"

Of course, Archie was all excited, leaving his seaweed-amber paw prints on her crisp jeans. I explained my situation, that I *loved* picking up the occasional bits of trash and that I had lost Archie's leash on a rock, and good thing I'd found the rope! She laughed and we sat on a bench and looked out at the whitecaps, dotted with colourful windsurfer sails and little black rubber figures being tossed into the dark green sea. The sky was full of kites and parasails. She told me that she had read a book about the death of the albatrosses off the coast of South America, and that when the oceanographers looked at the dead birds, they found that their innards were clogged with bottle caps.

Walking the wild beaches of Dallas Road is never boring, even though nothing much changes except the weather, which just goes to show that it is not a place or thing that amuses a person, but how you feel. I know that people go on great retreats to India or Tibet to learn this, but you don't need to—it's all right here on the Dallas Road beaches!

One of my most magnificent and memorable views of the sea from Dallas Road was in the autumn at sunset; it had been a clear, chilly day and the sun had just dipped below the horizon, leaving a golden glow that shimmered and skimmed the deep green and silver water—it left me breathless. I will never forget it—it was a Turner masterpiece.

But every so often, one does in fact come upon an unexpected change of sorts. One morning I was walking over the pebbles and thick twisted masses of kelp washed up from the previous night's high tide. Archie and I were the only ones on the beach. The oystercatchers were squeaking in the excitement of finding shellfish; a silent great blue heron stood like a mime, staring into a tidal pool. The gulls were drifting under a low grey sky above the cold black rocks. As I scrambled over the washed-in pile of bleached logs and stepped back down onto the smooth grey pebbles, I was stopped cold by what I saw—a drowned ram in his white wool, his elegant black face and stone eyes staring at the sky, his legs spread apart. The first thing I thought was, "How undignified." Had it been a human, I am not sure I could have passed him by, but an animal seems much nearer to nature than we do, so after a moment I calmed myself and hurried Archie along

Sooke Hills from Clover Point

too; he was sniffing curiously at the great mound of saturated wet wool.

It was the undignified position of the ram's rear legs that made him so vulnerable. (I feel the same way in my yoga class when we are "invited" to establish ourselves in a similar position.) It made me feel such pity for him, beyond the fact that he was drowned on a beach (he'd probably fallen from a cliff along the strait at Metchosin). His wide-open stance on his back, combined with his passive nature, lying there in the golden kelp and white shells and washed pebbles, was sad—he didn't look at rest, but simply tossed by the sea (which of course he was) and abandoned. It was more undignified than if the crows had pecked out his eyes; even the crows had ignored him.

That night, after Archie was asleep with his bone on his blanket at the foot of my bed, I soaked in a hot bath in an old-fashioned tub with legs. Then I lay in my cozy bed with my stack of books and I thought about the ram on the beach. A cool sea breeze blew in the little window. The street was quiet and there was a faint amber glow from the street light. The old lilac was rustling outside against the bathroom window, and I could smell the window sills and frames I had painted that morning—it was "eco paint," with a clean, light odour.

Bedtime is my favourite time of day. When I go to bed, everything seems to be clearer, including the memory of the day. I lay there in my cool cotton sheets and I thought, "I should have closed the ram's legs. I should have given him dignity." I decided to go to the beach in the morning and do that for him.

Then I remembered something that happened a long time ago, with Mum, when I was very young. It was a scorching-hot day in the New Brunswick countryside and we were walking along an old railway track with dry grass encroaching on the rusted rails. The intense dry heat had brought out the faint smell of the creosoted ties. Mum had a burlap sack and was looking for wild apples in the thick, dusty shrubbery—she made the best apple jelly, which dripped for days through cheesecloth hung between two chairs in our kitchen. Suddenly she turned to me in a momentary horror and said, "Anny, what's that under that bush?!" I bent down on the tracks and saw a huge, bloated, smooth grey body—it could have been a cow. I poked it with a stick as Mum stood back, speechless, but it turned out just to be a great boulder. It's a tiny memory, a moment in time with Mum that I will never forget—the horror on her face, the same, I am sure, as that I had when I saw the poor ram, a horror that perhaps comes with age.

The next morning, Archie and I made our way back to the little hidden beach. The grassy meadow at the top of the cliff was damp from an evening shower and by the time we went down the crumbling cement steps to the beach, Archie was wet and covered in flecks of oatmeal-coloured grass seeds. The sea mist was just dissipating into the white sky that hung low over the green sea, which was lapping and washing over the pebbles. We climbed over the slabs of granite and rock toward the place where the old ram rested amongst the sea debris and salt air. I thought as I climbed that if I had ever joined the Canadian Forces, I would have chosen the navy (Mum says they always had the nicest uniforms—she was a uniformed war artist in the army), so that if I were to be killed on duty, at least I would go back to the sea, the salty beautiful sea—perhaps eaten by some sea creature to be part of nature's food chain. I wonder what part of me would be the most tender. I wonder what part would actually taste the best.

Archie and I jumped down onto the white-washed shells and freshly washed-up smooth, amber kelp. There he was, the old ram, slightly shifted by the night tide but still intact, gazing in another direction. I thought, "All I should do is close his back legs—just pull one over," but I couldn't touch him. I was torn between which was more dignifying: to leave the body with nature, exposed and vulnerable, or to interfere and close it up? And I thought that if I knew only the sea and its creatures would see him, it would be okay to let him be, but it disturbed me that human beings might wander by and see him so undignified. That's what upset me and made me sad—animals wouldn't judge him but humans might.

A naked man was meditating farther out on the rock. At least, he *looked* naked. Archie ran out and sniffed him and I followed—I saw a piece of plastic just behind the man's (tanned and hairless, I noticed) buttocks. He was deep in thought—his eyes were closed and he was facing the Olympic Peninsula, a lovely snowcapped mountainous wilderness across the strait, in the United States. It's like a linear backdrop behind our sea, full of old-growth coniferous trees, hot springs, and cedar smells.

Mum always says that in the United States, "the coasts are so intelligent," but I would say that in Canada, the entire country is intelligent—we seem to be so much more bonded with intelligence, with modesty, and with a special compassion, and as much as it is at times frustrating, it is the right way to live. I am sure of that, because it is kind and positive, no matter how big we are. This, I think, is why we are in the greatest country in the world, and we should be secretly proud.

Well, back to the little beach where I scooped up the plastic within inches of the meditator. (One time Archie and I picked up beer cans around a person standing on her head, humming). My little inner voice held me back from repositioning the sad, water-sodden ram—I just couldn't do it.

Archie and I trundled home. A ferocious wind was picking up. Flags were flapping off porches, and freshly mown grass was blowing up the street. The old pinto horse pulling a carriage of tourists up our street bowed his head into the gale. The wind howled late into the night. Wind is a bit frightening, but I felt safer than I used to back on Glamorgan Farm, where I remember lying in my brass bed under the red tin roof, terrified that a huge cedar would come crashing down into the bedroom at any moment.

The next morning the street was scattered with debris and leaves. Archie and I took our beach walk, and I hoped that the old ram by this time had been swept out to sea forever. And sure enough, there was no sign of him, but rather, next to where he had been so exposed was a small bouquet of bluebells, lying limply on a black rock. My heart leapt in relief that compassion had been felt for the ram by another human being. Somebody else had paid their respects to his death.

Since then on our walks Archie and I have come across dead seals, gulls and one day a small fawn, its delicate mouth slightly open, amongst the washed-up kelp and seaweed. And the next day a little bouquet appeared on the carcass of a nearby log. Sometimes there is a small cairn of pebbles and shells, decorated with a feather or small pieces of driftwood. I add to the shrine, a bit of salty, blue sea glass or a scarlet leaf of seaweed. I do not wish to meet the secret shrine builder and fellow lover of life—I like the mystery, and I love knowing that there is somebody out there who is compassionate toward life. And I feel almost honoured to add to the little graves that appear mysteriously in the quiet dusk and dawn hours of the James Bay beaches.

In early autumn, the meadows along Dallas Road are a dry golden mass of wild oats and grasses, pale mauve asters, fireweed gone to seed, and thickets of bright orange rosehips. As Archie romps through this wildness, full of weeds and native plants with funny, naughty names such as bladder campion, hoary cress, and tansy ragwort, I think that nature is sometimes more beautiful in its ending stages, that the dying golden meadow is lovelier than its promising lushness months before.

On the slopes and bluffs, a mass of tumbling purple vetch fades into the sandy cliffs, and a ridge of yellow gorse on top dries to a brown, tangled, prickly mass. The thickets and random hedges are spotted orange with the Nootka rosehips in the meadow glades. I love the City for allowing the wildness of Mother Nature to put her meadows and thickets to sleep in the cool autumn sea air

in her own way. The friendly Victoria workers do just enough—they mow around a patch of asters, and push the beach logs back from the water just enough that we can walk along the shore without getting wet at winter's high tides. These workers have a lovely intuition for when pristine is not necessary.

When I was on the farm, I'd drift off in my little bedroom to the frog chorus and the faint smell of woodsmoke from the last embers of the fire in the wood stove in the kitchen. In James Bay I sometimes drift off to the same woodsmoke smell, but it comes from beach fires, which are not allowed but appear regularly anyway. Every so often a burning log will spark and set fire to the dry grasses of the bank, and then you hear the sirens of the fire trucks from the neighbourhood fire station down the road. The next day Archie and I will see blackened logs and grey ashes, sometimes still smouldering, amongst the beach stones. It's as if people really need to have a beach fire—for far *more* than just

warmth. Everything seems much more right in the world when we sit beside a beach fire. Then the glow from the ashes fades. After that, it's back to the harsh, cool world of reality. Fire seems to be an escape of some sort; perhaps it is even like a kind of purge, especially in the outdoors.

I don't know why the autumn, the "going to sleep season," brings on a time of reminiscence. Even the names of some of the wispy wet grasses that drape over my ankles and the dry seed pods that burst as I brush past them have farm-like names that make me remember the heavy autumn labour I did on Glamorgan Farm. Sow thistle, sheep sorrel, redroot pigweed, giant hogweed, jointed goatgrass—all wild and considered invasive, with names related to livestock! I wonder if these tough, invasive plants are named after livestock as a compliment or an insult.

The dying golden meadows and tangled invasives going to seed, the low grey skies, the empty beaches with remnants of beach fires washed by the cold sea bring on a certain melancholy, but at the same time a certain joy, a certain relief that a time of rest is approaching. The tides are suddenly higher, usually right after the Saanich Fair. The water is cold and clear, and thick blankets of voluptuous, emerald-green seaweed wash up over the beach like exotic dessert toppings. Beautiful, shimmering, deep-amber jellyfish float along the lapping shore, apparently migrating. What would be in a jellyfish

to tell it to migrate? How does it know? What did Mother Nature put into the jellyfish's mind to tell it to migrate? One may mock the idea that a jellyfish has a mind, but then, I would ask, what's the definition of a mind? And is a jellyfish's mind as harmful as the mind of a human who starts a war or commits a planned and cruel act?

How beautiful the jellyfish are! Their sparkling dark red glints through the cool water amongst the kelp and shells as their lacy outer frill taps the shoreline with each little wave. I read that the presence of jellyfish indicates a high level of nitrates in the water—pollution from chemicals. How ironic that something like toxic pollution can cause something so beautiful to occur! But of course the other theory is that they are simply seeking out a route. Who can read the mind of the beautiful jellyfish? One would ask them, "Beautiful jellyfish, are you here on Dallas Road just passing through, or are you here to eat nitrates?"

Other strange but beautiful sea creatures wash ashore in the autumn wind storms, such as the great Pacific chiton. When I first noticed these primitive-looking, burgundy-shelled humps in the kelp beds, I was quite intrigued. And when they were upside down (in that vulnerable position), they looked positively fleshy and, well, rather sexual. I am not really a sexual person, but a sexual thought crossed my mind! Those soft, oval, beige, benign and harmless creatures really looked like something out of a female-anatomy textbook, and they were the size of, say, a small football!

One cool winter's grey and drizzly day, tossed in the grey-green waves slapping against the black pebbles from the whitecapped sea, there was a shimmering mass of pink, and on a closer look I realized it was an octopus—its arms, lined with their distinctive white suckers, were limp and twisting gently in the rhythm of the waves. An ambitious seagull was trying to pull it to shore. The octopus was the same colour as the pink granite rocks that bounded the little bay.

I feel I must mention also the lowly sponge, although I have not seen a sponge washed up on our shores so far on my beach walks. We do have a lovely sponge in our waters called the yellow or lemon sponge. I mention sponges only because of a memory of a biology class I took thirty years ago. I had a tiny Asian instructor who was just learning English. She was describing the sponge's anatomy and said that a sponge uses the same cavity to take in food and release waste. "Sponge has no anus," she said seriously. "Sponge has only one hole for feeding and excretion, so moral of story is, never kiss a sponge." Well, I never forgot that! And it set me on a course of a lifelong interest in sea life.

If you'd like to see (and feed) the puppy-like harbour seals, the best place to go is Fisherman's Wharf, a charming part of James Bay on the Inner Harbour. It comprises a community of colourful floathouses (one is covered with salty "sea trash," including corroded cellphones obviously recovered from the local depths) and a flotilla of ice cream kiosks, cafés, kayak-rental outlets, seafood shops, and other ventures. One of the best ways to visit Fisherman's Wharf is to take one of the little Harbour Ferries from the main wharf off the lower causeway in the Inner Harbour.

These little tub-like boats, operated by retired sea captains, chug all around the harbour and stop at many interesting locations—heritage sites, pubs, parks, and walkways. It's a delightful way to see the city and its waterfront neighbourhoods, and in the summer months, on Sundays, the boats perform a "waltzing water ballet" to the music of Strauss in the harbour, which you can see from the cool stone wall above the causeway while enjoying an ice cream or lemonade. It's very comical but also endearing, seeing these grown men (some of whom were probably at one time in the navy fighting sea battles) manoeuvring their little boats in unison between gleaming, expensive yachts, with the float planes coming in to land overhead.

One morning Archie and I were alone on our beach walk; washed up on the shore with a fish head was a small corked bottle. The bottle had no label and was murky from its time in the salt water. Well, you won't believe this, but there was a message in the bottle! This is what it said, written with good penmanship:

Please to be helping me!
First I say free Tibet, now made I
to make glass bottles in factory as
prisoner!
I doctor not see family in 4 years.
Help Please!!

Do you think this could be a joke? These words were followed by some Chinese writing, which I plan to decipher with the help of a friend in Chinatown. The paper seemed very new and white, not what I would think Chinese paper from China would be like. In the end there was no contact information, so there was little to be done, but the exercise certainly made me think and wonder.

I wonder why it's so exciting to find a message in a bottle. Every time I see a bottle in the ocean, my heart leaps and I think, "I wonder if there's a message in it." Is it the anticipation of making a strange and new contact in the world with the sea as our mediator? I think it would be far more interesting to meet friends in this way than on Facebook. Maybe the computer, with all its speed and instant answers, and Facebook with all its "friends," are taking away our thrill of anticipation, of waiting and wondering and hoping, of imagining a wonderful outcome, which may be found in a message in a bottle.

In the summer, on warm Saturday nights, movies are shown outdoors in Beacon Hill Park. Residents of the surrounding neighbourhood, most wearing their pyjamas, stroll up the streets carrying blankets, cans of popcorn, folding chairs, and thermoses of coffee. We traipse over the medieval-looking stone bridge and converge under the great oak and maple canopy in front of a huge blow-up screen at the bandstand, an old stage painted pale green, which sits in a grassy dell surrounded by ancient, wild, pink rhododendrons and towering firs that house a massive number of blue-heron nests. The eagles and other raptors get some of the baby herons, but I have noticed that there are definitely more herons in the park and on the beach. We hunker down, all of us strangers, in our blankets under a cool, starry sky to watch old Pee-wee Herman and Muppet movies as the park peacocks and mallards settle down to rest for the night.

There's something very special that bonds together strangers and neighbourhood residents on movie nights—I think it's the fact that we are all wearing pyjamas in a public place. When we're wearing pyjamas, we are all one step closer together, not naked, but all acknowledging that we are ready for our bedtime. It's something all

humans have in common—the desire to unwind, to sleep, to go through this nighttime ritual of wearing pyjamas and watching a movie with popcorn under a warm blanket, and that's what happens on summer Saturday nights in Beacon Hill Park: the nonverbal closeness of bedtime.

Just on the edge of James Bay, quite near Dallas Road and across the road from Beacon Hill Park where a statue of Terry Fox and Mile Zero look out to sea, is the historic Beacon Drive In, which first opened in 1958. The café, with its yellow awnings and painted menu outside and its green vinyl booths and bad lighting inside, became famous for its soft ice cream; those were the days when there was great comfort in licking an ice cream and strolling around the park's ponds under the shady maple trees and through the rose garden. It is still very much a comfort. On warm summer days, the lineup for ice cream and burgers goes around the corner and into the alley.

Apart from walking Archie along the Dallas Road beaches and through the park, I regularly visit James Bay Coffee and Books, full of used books and with local art on its walls. The wooden tables are covered in green plastic tablecloths and are surrounded by musty old, yellowed, cellophane-covered books about nature and history and local heritage, many illustrated with faded watercolour sketches and charming ink

Sea Life off Dallas Road

What is it about the Victoria coastline? It turns out that the jellyfish and the chiton I found washed up on the beach on an autumn day are the largest of their species in the world! People who love jellyfish refer to them affectionately as "jellies." The beautiful amber jellies that I discovered on the beach turned out to be lion's mane jellyfish. They can be over six feet across, with sixty-five-foot tentacles; they pulsate along our coastline—the big ones are in the colder northern waters. They have a one-year lifespan, which explains why they end up on the shore regularly (yearly). And apparently they can still sting when they are dead! (One suggestion for treating the sting is to use vinegar). When jellies reproduce, they enter a polyp phase—little polyps reproduce and stack up, then develop and swim off.

Now our red chiton is a primitive mollusc and can grow to over a foot in length! The giant Pacific chiton is also known as the "gumboot chiton" because it truly looks like the thick rubber sole of a gumboot. It is also known as "the wandering meatloaf," which I think is a bit of an insult.

The chiton's shell is composed of numerous plates, called butterfly shells because they are butterfly-shaped. Our great chiton therefore is sometimes referred to as "the coat of mail," which is much kinder than "meatloaf"—it sort of gives it a knighthood! The word *chiton* is Greek for "tunic," which can apply to the chiton's fashionable shell; it is rather toga-like and clings to its soft, beige body. I felt sad for the chiton when it was upside down on the shore—it seemed so vulnerable, its soft tissue exposed to the world and its armour, its only protection, facing the earth.

This old, odd creature can live for forty years as it clings to the sea rocks and eats algae and sea lettuce at night. Red algae may give this chiton the burgundy colour of its shell and plates. Our great winter storms can knock the chiton off its rocks, so that's why it often ends up in the kelp beds on our shores, upside down for all the world to see.

Why do creatures seem so much more vulnerable when they are on their backs? Is it because they are helpless in that position? Is that position, to us, more undignified? We might wonder why it is not a position of strength and pride and openness and freedom, and therefore power and courage, when a heart faces the universe, the sun, and the heavens. Why do we feel more secure facedown?

The giant Pacific octopus, another creature we have here, is the largest in the world. The octopus has eight arms; that explains the "octo," but what about the "pus"? Though our octopus is a mollusc, it does not have a hard protective shell, which means it can squeeze into a rock shelf or crevice easily for protection or to lay eggs. There are two hundred and eighty sensitive suckers on each arm, which grab hold of food; the octopus has a strong beak (mouth) and a barbed tongue that can crack open a shell for a feast.

Our octopus is colour-blind, but, ironically, it can change colours easily as a defence against predators. Imagine being able to blend in with your surroundings when you're nervous! How many times have we wished

we could do the same thing? The octopus can blend into a rock or a bed of seaweed. If I were nervous, say, downtown, for example, I would love to be able to blend into a shelf of calendars in a bookshop, or a glassed-in display of tarts and cakes in a coffee shop!

A great part of the octopus's body is enclosed in the "mantle," a sack-like structure that contains his organs, including three hearts. (His blood is a pale blue—he's a "blue-blood," like the monarchy!) Our giant Pacific octopus is also very intelligent. Tests have been done in which the octopus actually figured out how to open a jar and go through a maze (in a lab). This endears our slimy pink marine friend to me—not only is he smart, but he was made to prove it.

The final fact about our dear octopus is how they lovingly care for their young. The female lays her eggs and spends months caring for them, cleaning and protecting them, and then she quietly dies—her duty is done. The males die as well, after they breed. The lifespan of our octopus is short, from three to five years.

drawings. There is never any pressure to leave or to rush, and on Tuesday evenings the locals gather for Scrabble nights. (Did you know that *qa* is an accepted word? And so is *em*—that's how you spell the letter *M*! They are in the Scrabble dictionary but not in Webster's.) On Friday nights the place is lit up for an "open mike" where locals can get up and sing, followed by a featured performer. The event is hosted by a lovely, happy, smiling woman with a grand sense of humour as she announces the acts in front of the old wooden bookcases crammed with self-help books and historical novels.

The bulletin board is full of colourful ads for psychic readings, massage therapy, and spiritual solutions to the many problems that ail us. The place smells of old wood and plaster, simmering soup, brewing coffee, old books, and herbal oils (which are most likely on the patrons).

I love books, and I think you can love books more than you can love reading them. What is it about books that is so appealing? They are like little condensed works of art—thoughts on paper rather than in one's imagination (maybe when something is written, it becomes more real). And I love the

Dallas Road in Snow

Every so often it snows in Victoria! It's a great event; even with two inches, the schools and businesses usually close for the day, and the gentle slope at Beacon Hill Park is dotted with little figures in red snowsuits tobogganing down toward the sea.

On one snowy walk, Archie and I tromped along the beach early in the morning. The winter dawn was a sight to behold. There were three continuous ribbons— the deep, frigid, mineral-grey-green sea, the black strip of pebbles, and the white snow above. The only colour was a little smudge of yellow under the snow on the beach—a frozen bouquet of chrysanthemums, left in memory of someone who loved the sea. One light shone dimly, far out on the misty winter ocean, from a lone tanker.

coziness of books, just like the coziness of a fire in a wood stove. I care very much for the environment and believe in saving trees and paper, but my heart is pulled toward the cozy and comfy feelings that books and fireplaces provide—between us, the coziness wins over my conscience.

That is why I think books and bookshops, especially used-book stores, will always be with us, because we innately crave the comfort, and I pity humanity if we ever lose that need. And that's why electronic books will never replace paper books, because you cannot display electronic books, and there's no aesthetic delight for our senses with electronic books. Come to think of it, oral story-telling will never fully disappear either. If it did, that would be one step toward shutting down our imaginations, which, I suppose, human beings may choose to do (to not tell stories), but it would be a shame. It might mean the demise of a type of creative and philosophical thought that has occupied us for centuries, since humans first decorated their caves or carved pieces of bone.

Well, back to my coffee shop. I found a book about hedgerows, which I thumbed through with a cappuccino. Slightly mildewed with yellowed and musty-smelling pages, it had numerous illustrations of shrubbery and hedgehogs and hares and other wildlife under berry bushes. The hedgerows of today in our urban neighbourhoods and rural areas are composed of natural growing trees,

shrubs, and wildflowers. They still provide protection from wind and erosion and also supply food and habitat for country wildlife and pollen for bees in our region.

In some ways, James Bay is like a used-book store—a place of great heritage, a quirky haven full of tales, musty secrets and remnants, with a treasure here and there.

Cook Street Village

CHAPTER TWO

Fairfield, Cook Street Village, and Rockland

Fairfield is a lovely neighbourhood just along the beach from James Bay. The very name Fairfield evokes country pleasure, fresh air, and urban charm. Fairfield is an old English place name from *fair* which means "beautiful," and *feld* which means "open country." James Douglas, the second governor of Vancouver Island, owned a large, rambling estate just east of James Bay, and he named it Fairfield.

Cook Street Village is an ambling portion of Fairfield. The huge shady canopy of horse chestnut trees that lines the village provides you with a feeling of rest, of being able to slow down and have a coffee at an ornate little metal table on the sidewalk and know that at that moment, you are content and happy within your world. You may be able to feel a little state of bliss in Cook Street Village. It's a free and easy street, tucked between the wild open sea at the bottom and the bustling downtown at the top, a linear rest stop between two opposing forces.

Cook Street is of course named for our hero, Captain James Cook, who charted our coastline in the late 1700s. There's a statue of him on the Inner Harbour, and he looks quite handsome and also sensitive. It seems odd that a statue can cause me to feel for the man because of his looks—I think it's the neat little curled ponytail tied with a ribbon, and his slim calves, and the elegant way he stands. It makes him seem vulnerable, somehow. I'm sure if he had been given pudgy calves or loose, billowing hair, I wouldn't feel for him so. His elegance and dignity are extremely attractive.

Cook Street Village is a strolling and unwinding place where you can take your dear dogs into the Pic A Flic video store (it's SPCA recognized!) and spend hours selecting a film on almost any topic. As you browse for a video on the life of Chagall or a classic like Bette Davis's *What Ever Happened to Baby Jane?* your wet, hairy, exhausted, panting dog can lie on the carpet after a huge run at the nearby beach.

And there's a butcher shop, Island Meat & Seafood, which sells meat that has been humanely raised and not fed chemicals or growth hormones. People who walk and shop on Cook Street are pleased about this. They are residents with common sense who need to know that the pork they are going to eat didn't live in a crowded piggery and wasn't fed antibiotics. Oh, the history of the pig as a mass-consumer item is just too sad to think about!

The side streets are just as peaceful, with charming and quaint wooden two-storeyed houses, attic windows painted in lemons, greys, creams, and soft teals, glassed-in verandas and pretty porches, well-pruned tea roses and espaliered apple trees neatly climbing cedar trellises. But there are enough differences between the houses to make an interesting and varied streetscape. The homeowners around Cook Street have a type of genteel taste, and an appreciation of nature and gardens (many have "taken the pledge" to go pesticide-free) and a knowledge of how fresh laundry smells when it's hung out in the air to dry.

At Halloween, the jack-o'-lanterns in Fairfield are neatly carved into spooky faces of ghosts with toothless grins, which sit on porch railings and in big stained-glass windows and then, after the frightening night, are taken to the community compost centre. (In James Bay, the pumpkins are carved with sails, hearts, stars, and moons, and placed in apple trees and lawn sculptures. After Halloween many carved pumpkins appear on the great logs on the beach, and the sea gulls have a feast before the winter's grey tide washes them away and they become one with the sea glass and kelp.)

Men with shoulder satchels stroll through Cook Street Village, some wearing rolled-up black jeans, others in lime-green ski jackets and pants with side pockets. Cook Street is all about the stroll. Many merchants move their wares outside onto the sidewalk, so people are forced to amble. When merchandise, especially interesting items such as lovely blue cotton rag rugs, vintage clothing, organic soaps, art books, and trolleys of herbs are displayed on the sidewalk, a barrier is broken down between the shop and the walker. Shop owners sweep the sidewalks and greet passersby. They are putting themselves "out there" as part of the strolling community, and that's very appealing for a pleasurable amble through a village. This sense of pride in the merchants flows onto the streets—add a dog dish of water, large pots of pansies, pretty awnings fluttering in the ocean breeze, freshly painted sandwich boards, red-enamel bike racks, Sunday papers, and quaint little restaurants that sell oven-baked pizza and herbal teas or mochas, and we have the village experience.

There's a lot to be said for pride, and for taste, and for good old-fashioned community. Cook Street in essence resembles a traditional old English

village—the philosophy is that the little shops are an everyday experience for people who live nearby. Perhaps its appeal to the public beyond the area is that by strolling through the village, they feel a part of the immediate community.

There are no art galleries with broad glass windows displaying rich oil paintings of landscapes and still lifes in gold-leaf frames under strategically placed spotlights; none that offer wine and cheese and chocolate gingers on art openings where you can read the artist's statement (most of which I rarely understand) in a glossy pamphlet. Rather, artists in the Cook Street area sell their art from their homes, lovely homes with stepping-stone pathways, woolly thyme, and pots of tulips on the porch in spring.

East of Cook Street Village, on nearby Moss Street, is one of Victoria's busiest and most popular Saturday street markets held throughout the summer. Perhaps one sign of a city's coming of age is that it has a daily market, but for now the Cook Street area can boast of a healthy, vibrant, weekly market, set up under an array of little white tents in the Sir James Douglas schoolyard,

where people amble, carrying woven Peruvian baskets to fill with everything from exotic mushrooms, orange beets, and homemade cilantro salsa to jars of chutney and other lovely concoctions such as Bartlett Pear Butter With Vanilla.

One farmer had a basket of quince for sale. The pale yellow, smooth-skinned quince, lightly covered with a soft down, always reminds me of a teenage boy's face (not the yellow part but the fuzziness). The quince is an old fruit, hard as rock but delicious when stewed or made into jelly. We don't see it very often anymore, so it is delightful to know that it has been kept popular by a farmer at the Moss Street Market. A delicious way to serve quince for dessert is simply to bake it and then add a little maple syrup to sweeten it, and some whipped cream and maybe a tiny sprinkle of nutmeg.

One of the largest stands at the Moss Street Market is the apple kiosk. Here the vendor, from a nearby Gulf Island, sets out numerous wooden boxes of apples, all different sizes and colours, and because he doesn't spray with pesticides and other poisons, his wonderful country apples look like the fruit that our grandmothers grew—with blemishes and spots and not perfectly round!

These apples aren't only clean and organic, but many are of heirloom varieties. A sign listing the country of origin and date sits in every box: "1809—Bramley—England"; "1750—King—New Jersey"; "1790—Esopus [that's a place in New York] Spitzenburg." I bought the oldest heirloom, a 1740 Blenheim Orange from England. There were tasting plates as well, and it was great fun to compare the tartness and textures of these dear old species. One of the most intriguing was the "Pink Delight—Origin Unknown." It was a sweet apple with bright pink flesh, probably a creation by Mother Nature (she alone knows the real origin), crossbreeding her old heirlooms in a wild orchard on a breezy day when the pollen flew around and landed where it preferred. Or it may have been the work of a busy honeybee making its rounds.

East of Moss Street and a little ways along the shore is historic Ross Bay Cemetery. Apart from

Gonzales Bay

and this area is regularly cordoned off with orange sandwich boards and yellow plastic tape while workers put the road and property back together. These brutal storms literally washed the dead out of their graves and were part of the reason the Chinese graves in this part of the cemetery were moved to a more peaceful meadow on higher ground in nearby Oak Bay back in 1903 (see Chapter Three).

You can take guided Sunday-afternoon walking tours of the Ross Bay Cemetery with guides from the Old Cemeteries Society (tour groups meet across the road at the mall), and the interesting tours are usually theme-based. Cemeteries are not only about the deceased; they are also cultural landscapes. The Old Cemeteries Society has published some very informative brochures, which include a description of many of the graves at Ross Bay; you can visit the graves of Emily Carr, some of the Sisters of St. Ann, the Dunsmuir family (the famous coal barons), and Victoria Jane Wilson, who left her inherited wealth to her pet parrot to supply him with brandy, his favourite drink!

We cannot leave Fairfield without mentioning the Art Gallery of Greater Victoria and Government House Gardens, both located in Rockland, an area of wide, shady, tree-lined avenues with spacious lawns in front of large heritage homes and sprawling but neatly pruned blooming shrubbery and old rock walls.

The art gallery is housed in a Queen Anne-style

containing the graves of many well-known, historically important people from Victoria's past, the cemetery is also known as a windblown place where winds lash the edge of the property with salt, sleet, driftwood logs, sand, and anything else that blows up from the beaches in our winter storm season. The winds often blow down trees and whip the waves right over parts of the road—it's very dramatic, mansion, which was built in 1889 and is painted in traditional heritage colours (a bright pinkish-orange with deep jade-green trim). Although the gallery has a large permanent collection of works by Emily Carr and the Group of Seven, the focus is on Asian art, and it has an Asian-themed garden that includes, amongst the Japanese maples, pink dogwoods, and bamboos, an authentic Shinto shrine. Inside the gallery is a huge iron bell (1641) from China's Ming dynasty.

Many Japanese plants do very well in Victoria because our climate is similar to that of parts of Japan, but philosophically and historically, our gardens do differ. Even though our Victoria gardeners love to manicure our shrubs and train them to travel sideways, we do have a wild side! Our deep rainforests laden with fern, fungi and moss, our windswept meadows of gnarled Garry oak, our old orchards, sand-beaten grassy estuaries and seashores, are quite untamed and often make up local landscapes within our region and within our neighbourhoods. But in Japan, perhaps because it is smaller, control of the vegetation, such as the practice of bonsai, seems much more important. There is a bonsai display at the art gallery—wildness repressed—and even a bonsai salal shrub.

I took the drop-in tour to see

the ancient Chinese pottery exhibit, a collection of vases, dishes, and trinkets with beautiful glazes and patterns retrieved from old shipwrecks off China's shores. A man in a tweed suit and a name tag guided our small group around a white room filled with Plexiglas boxes displaying ancient, salt-encrusted teapots, jugs, and opium containers. On the walls hung old British oil paintings of stormy seascapes with clipper ships being tossed in the grey ocean, but I noticed that in every picture, there was a narrow and subtle strip of hopeful and promising yellow sunshine far away on the horizon.

One of the more elegant and exquisite pieces of pottery was what looked like a tiny chamber pot, but in fact it was a "vomit pot." (I had never heard of such a thing, but it was the most beautiful piece of pottery I have ever seen—how ironic that it had such a not-so-pretty use!)

I happened to visit the gallery once on a dark, drizzly, blustery autumn day, and it was a lovely thing to do. I browsed the Persian miniature paintings that depict everyday life, such as miniature gold-leaf scenes of a shepherd in a red smock tending his flock of grazing goats. It was charming as the wind outside whipped the slim red leaves off the Japanese maples around the Shinto shrine.

Government House

Near the art gallery stands our stately Government House, residence of our lieutenant-governors. All sorts of ceremonial government events take place throughout the year that are open to the public. One of the most moving ceremonies is the swearing-in of new Canadians; there is something so compassionate about our country taking in new citizens, welcoming them to our home to begin new lives. I think that's what multiculturalism and compassion are all about, and compassion permeates the Canadian cultural landscape.

Another striking feature of the ceremonies is the military-style clothing that our lieutenant-governor wears. Oh, it's magnificent and regal, with swirling gold braiding and slim-fitting coattails and a beautiful hat with a white plume.

Although this beautiful historic building is worth visiting, it is the restored gardens on the thirty-five acres, set amongst the Garry oaks and camas meadows, that prove to be a grand highlight. The gardens are open to the public every day of the year, and in the warmer months there are picnics and games and tea and musical concerts on the lawn. The gardens are tended by four hundred volunteers! The volunteers even hold fundraisers to buy the plants, which they spend hours putting into the many beautiful beds. It is estimated that these dedicated volunteers save the provincial government close to a million dollars in labour by caring for these vast and varied gardens.

Composting is done on site, and there are beehives to supply honey for special occasions. Vegetables and fruit are also grown for use within the household. There are rose gardens, heather gardens, rock and alpine gardens, and water gardens, and benches for resting and pathways for strolling. Although they contain some exotic plants from faraway lands, including the Chinese dogwood, Mediterranean lavender, and the Cape fuchsia from South Africa, the gardens at Government House are not botanical gardens for educational purposes but are, rather, a source of beauty and serenity for us all to enjoy.

Credit for the garden restoration and expansion is given to Lieutenant-Governor David Lam, who took office in 1988. He apparently donated his entire salary toward the project! The gardens actually were established back in 1911 but over the years had fallen into disrepair and neglect. When I look at our community now, I see, more than ever before, a positive recognition of the need to restore and preserve the beauty of the past and to create present and future beauty as well, and this is thanks to sensitive and forward-thinking people like Mr. Lam and these volunteers.

The efforts and love the volunteers put into this beautiful landscape give me great hope.

Willows Tea Room at Oak Bay

CHAPTER THREE

Oak Bay

Oak Bay, named after the many old oak trees that line the quiet streets and are spread across the wild parks and meadows, is known for its Englishness, and indeed there are some features that are very British, such as tea houses and a pub called The Penny Farthing. But when I walked through the absolutely stunningly beautiful camas and Garry oak meadows in Uplands Park, the *people* were more English than the landscape. The scenery and physical features are quite Canadian, but it is the people who reflect the Englishness of Oak Bay. I was passed by energetic older residents who carried walking sticks and wore tweed caps and tall buckled gumboots, accompanied by wet Labrador dogs with lolling pink tongues.

Oak Bay has some unique features that are clearly not English; did you know that it is "The Palm Tree Capital of Canada"? The palm-tree count in 2006 was 2,669! There's even a self-guided tour you can take to see the palm trees, some of which are thirty feet high.

With English gardens characteristically known for precise pruning and planned landscape design, Oak Bay's Native Plant Garden on Beach Avenue stands as another unique feature that breaks the mould of Englishness. The land was donated by Ada G. Beaven (1867–1958) and is lovingly tended by the local Native Plant Society. It's a lush pocket oasis with shafts of sunlight illuminating groves of burgundy trilliums, ferns, fawn lilies, and bluebells under the green shade of Indian plum, snowberry, maples, and evergreens. A dear little winding chip path takes you on a gentle curved stroll through this delightful native woodland, where logs are allowed to rot back into the earth, weeds are not weeds but a food source for birds and insects, and slugs can wander freely.

Tea at nearby Willows Beach is like being in

an era gone by. The tea house on the beach is a simple white structure with blue trim, originally built in 1949. Its salt-sprayed windows overlook the promenade, with its dark green hand railing, along the vast stretch of sand, and inside the tables are covered with white plastic table cloths adorned with tiny bouquets of *real* pink carnations. You can have chips or tea or an ice cream and a few other snacks. The tea house is run by volunteers for the Oak Bay Kiwanis Club; they are raising money for one of their many compassionate causes, a residential care home for the elderly that will include a therapeutic garden and a van for venturing out on local excursions.

A particularly charming part of Oak Bay is its village, which is lined not only with little shops but also numerous art galleries. The streetscape of Oak Bay Village is bustling, colourful, and joyous, with pretty street banners on freshly painted lampposts—shiny black with gold oak leaves—potted plants shaded by shop awnings, hanging flower baskets, and informative heritage plaques. The shops are small and low, no more than two storeys, so you can always see the sun through the tops of the trees. The original 1936 Oak Bay Village sign sways above the sidewalk where a little theatre stood in the 1930s—admission was ten cents. The oldest business is the Oak Bay hardware store, which has been there since 1912.

The village is known to have a very British flair, and it does in fact have many English features; you can purchase British newspapers at Ivy's Bookshop and have a meat pie at The Penny Farthing, but what is on the increase in Oak Bay Village are the delectable and elegant food outlets. There's The Village Butcher, a shop run by a man considered an artisan with meat—he makes two kinds of the most delicious pepperoni I have ever tasted—and there's Ottavio's, an Italian deli and bakery where you can pick up lemon polenta, aged Tuscan sheep cheese, bourbon bread pudding, fig shortbread, or Italian truffle butter. There's Feys and Hobbs across the street, where a fine cup of coffee comes on a wooden platter accompanied by a little jug of cream. All the Feys and Hobbs products are made locally from local ingredients; the crackers are actually handmade, and you can also buy bacon jam and suffins, a delicious bun that is a combination of a muffin and a scone. Feys is the owner, and Hobbs is his dog. Oak Bay Village may have its British flavour, but as one merchant explained to me, it is becoming a "foodie mecca."

The municipal hall displays local art and heritage photographs of the old streetcars, which is a refreshing change from the dimly lit, dull-beige buildings with blank walls you must usually endure when paying a utility bill or asking the location of the gas lines under your front lawn. Perhaps our municipal halls should indeed be cultural centres; they certainly would be more inviting to

Oak Bay Avenue

do business in! Oak Bay loves its heritage; it still has manhole covers that date back to the 1800s, imported from Scotland and used as ballast in sailing ships.

Everywhere you look in Oak Bay there is a plaque, a cairn, or a kiosk describing a historical aspect of the place. At wild and windswept but beautiful Cattle Point, there is a brass plaque explaining that the land used to be part of the Hudson's Bay Company's farm and that from 1860 to 1910, cattle were barged from the mainland and pushed overboard to swim ashore, where cowboys would round them up; I don't think the poor cows' swim would be as traumatic as trying to scale the black, jagged, rocky shore.

At nearby Uplands Park, a cairn that overlooks the sea is dedicated to Walter M. Walker (1887–1983), an Oak Bay councillor who had the brilliant idea of creating the seventy-five-acre park, a place of stunning beauty where the rich bluish-purple camas in the spring sunshine actually hurt your eyes from their beauty. Sometimes beauty actually physically hurts from its intensity. It's not often that art can provide the same intensity nature does, although there are some pieces of music that can bring me to tears, such as Elgar's "Enigma Variations."

My awe and wonder at the stunning Garry oak meadow in Uplands Park were interrupted on one visit by a woman who was marching and lunging in her Lycra pants and pink visor, blowing and puffing erratically along the grassy paths and bringing her knees up to her pale chin with every elongated stride. It reminded me of John Cleese in the Monty Python skit about the Ministry of Silly Walks. I wondered if she knew how beautiful a camas flower is.

Closer to Oak Bay Village there is a large green space called Windsor Park. It's simply a spacious soccer field with a clubhouse in the centre, but when you stand there, it does look definitely British and I questioned why, as it is just a field, and then I realized that it is the design, the use and placement of space, that gives the park its English look; the clubhouse, a long two-storey tan structure, stands in the *centre* of the great space, not at one end. The vastness of the mowed field adds to the vision that a grand school cricket or rugby championship match is about to take place. Low, attractive houses surround the park on all four sides with one corner of white, Tudor-style connected shops serving as a quaint village centre.

One corner of Windsor Park is a dear little "scented garden"

Garry Oaks

Although the statuesque Garry oak is unique in that it grows only in this area of the world (from California to Victoria—a few are seen north of Nanaimo), and it is British Columbia's only native oak, the wonderful feature about the tree is not actually the tree, but its surroundings, its meadow— there is nothing quite like a Garry oak meadow in spring! When the Garry oak's leaves burst into their lush and glossy greenery, the meadow is a carpet of camas, buttercups, lilies, meadow herbs, and delicate pink shooting stars. Dry, golden, weathered lichen covers granite rock faces that sit like islands in the colourful grass and floral carpet. These unique and special features attract specific birds, insects and little animals such as the alligator lizards who like to bask on the warmed rock.

Garry oak acorns can be eaten after soaking them in mud to remove the bitter tannins (however, my dear old sows on the farm spat the acorns from their slop in disgust). Legend has it that if you carry the acorn around with you, your youthfulness will be preserved!

with lavender, lemon mint, and lilac growing from waist-high stone beds. A plaque in Braille indicates that the garden is for the visually impaired. Sometimes I wonder what our sensitivity to touch or sound would be if we were blind—imagine feeling all the textures of leaves, flowers, and even bark without seeing them!

In the other corner of the park is a rose garden protected by a neatly trimmed hedge and a little metal gate. Inside are neat garden beds of many types of roses; there is the Leonardo Da Vinci Floribunda, the Betty Boop, and the Burgundy Iceberg. At one end is a polished granite bench engraved with a tribute to the "Oak Bay pioneers since 1911" from Robert C. Pattison (1886–1963), the Oak Bay druggist, and "his devoted wife Rose."

On my visit to the Monterey Centre, a spacious community centre with an endless list of diverse courses for the members to take, a jar of freshly picked flowers sat on a table in front of a poster advertising a course on the Royal Family. The centre

has a large number of volunteers and you can buy, for a very reasonable price, a delicious homemade lunch of lamb stew, which comes with a roll. But the feature that most stands out in my mind is the tapestry on a back wall in a hallway, almost swamped by bookcases and shelves, sewn in 1977 by Dorita Grant. It depicts the different heritage structures of Oak Bay (and their dates) in shades of blue and brown wool. There's the Willows Hotel of 1904, the Oak Bay Boat House of 1906, and "The Old Charming Inn" of 1905, among others; it's original and delightful and what fun it must have been to sew! To me, that's a real piece of public art, and it was donated.

Close to Fairfield, out on Harling Point, sits the Chinese Cemetery, a National Historic Site. The austere and treeless wildflower meadow looks out over the sea at the white peaks of the Olympic Peninsula. The cemetery was established in 1903 by the Chinese Benevolent Society and designed according to the Chinese concept of feng shui, a three-thousand-year-old philosophy based on energy, nature, and balance within a space. It's a good system, I think, because I have been in places where I was truly uncomfortable, where the place just felt not right, and I know of some places that continually have bad occurrences; maybe these places need feng shui.

Feng means "wind" and *shui* means "water," and both are associated with good fortune and good health. So the placement of the simple aged stones and marble slabs, and the tall double altar where people can leave candy, oranges, and paper money and burn incense to say a prayer or honour a deceased loved one, stands according to the Earth's feeling within the space of this windswept, beautiful meadow. The altar looks vulnerable, standing out there all alone, but it also looks strong. Perhaps that is the point: vulnerability and strength, opposite sides of the same coin, the yin and the yang.

An ancient Chinese practice was to exhume the bones of the deceased after seven years, wash them, pack them in a crate, and send them home to China for reburying. While awaiting shipping, the bones were stored in a little hut called a "bone house" (now destroyed). This practice ended in 1933 but is an important part of the cemetery's history.

Behind the cemetery is a little country lane of weather-beaten cottages with salt-stained glassed-in porches and wind-battered climbing roses, almost begging to be allowed to revert back to wildness, clinging onto their trellises. This little lane seems to be out of another era (like the Willows Beach tea house), a gentle buffer between the quiet, harmonious cemetery meadow and our modern urban civilization just up the slope and a block away.

Perhaps this is the Oak Bay that is so appealing. Its rural charm, which is a mixture of camas meadows, bluebell woods, and breathtaking seaside views, is combined with the urban village, the

pruned gardens, and lectures on Prince William—it's the yin-yang again, the wildness and the tamed, the strong and the vulnerable, the British and our Canadian west coast.

Government Street at Belleville

CHAPTER FOUR

Lower Government Street and a Little Beyond

Lower Government Street (the area around the Inner Harbour and the Empress Hotel) is a hub of urban, cultural, marine, and residential activity, full of buskers and carvers, artisans, cafés, gardens, and many little historical and traditional features to explore. Lower Government Street borders the east of James Bay, running right from the beaches of Dallas Road all the way to the charming downtown area.

Let's begin at Emily Carr's birthplace, her elegant, canary-yellow heritage home, now a museum with a lovely English garden full of primroses and lilies, and a cozy, traditional interior. In Michael Ostroff's film about Emily Carr, *Winds of Heaven*, it is noted that her British father thought the Canadian landscape too wild and untamed, so he quickly uprooted the west-coast vegetation of ferns and forest shrubbery and created his fragrant and pretty English country

garden to suit his very British taste! Nowadays, the trend is to plant a native plant garden, but I have to admit that a mass of Canterbury bells, sweet Williams, snapdragons, and tea roses is aesthetically more stimulating than a mass of sword ferns and creeping blackberry in a front garden. Perhaps it is innate, this desire we have for colour and garden scents; perhaps we actually need colour in our lives.

Alas, however, Emily loved the woods and wildness—she found colour in the shafts of sunlight in the rainforest, the big night skies and how the forest made her feel; you do not always need to agree with your parents' tastes. She did try to be English with her little watercolour landscapes of the Beacon Hill meadow, dotted with spring flowers, and pale blue seascapes.

Walking (in spring under a sweet-smelling canopy of pale pink flowers) toward town from

Emily's house, you pass the historic red-brick-and-plaster James Bay Inn, established in 1911. If you like staying in places of yesteryear, this inn is for you; the lobby smells a bit musty in a lovely old way—a combination of aged wood and home cooking from downstairs—and the trimmings are in red velvet, brass, and heavy glass, with antique photographs in thick wooden frames. There is something comforting about an old hotel with uneven floors that creak and a worn carpet, heavy, cast-iron bathtubs with legs, and keys rather than computer cards to lock the doors (the key gives us so much more manual control of our privacy), and curtains, which are so much less sterile than blinds, and windows that open. Heaven preserve us from protecting ourselves by giving ourselves recycled air and windows that won't open on the seventh floor in a beige box with a fibreglass bathtub.

This old hotel is one of the last symbols that respects our common sense and judgment, allows us to take the risk of not falling out of an open window and allows us to breathe nature's air and scents from the outdoors. The soundproofing may not be as solid as in the great beige towers, but I find it a great delight to drift off to sleep with the muffled sounds of joy coming from the street or the dining room

three floors below—it's like going to sleep as a child with the security of hearing your parents' voices downstairs, chatting in the warm kitchen.

A little farther along, on the corner, is what all the neighbourhoods in Victoria have: the corner store. What a delight this particular one is! It is called The Birdcages Walk Confectionary because it was near here that the first government buildings, nicknamed "The Birdcages," were built.

The Birdcages corner store has a red awning covering neat rows of pails full of daffodils and tulips in spring, carnations, lilies, iris, freesias, and mums most of the year, huge golden sunflowers and dahlias in the autumn, and holly and green festive bouquets in winter. Inside there is a warm red glow—the little shop is crammed with boxes of candies, racks of postcards, glass vases, newspapers, toiletries, lavender incense, and even a potted orchid! Photographs of local customers and the neighbourhood are pinned above a cluttered shelf of paper bags of nuts and seeds for the birds in nearby Beacon Hill Park.

I think there are several things that give this corner store such charm. One is that it is indeed a *part* of the neighbourhood community, hence the selling of bird food, and the corner store is always *there*, like the CBC and *The Globe and Mail*; even on the worst stormy day, you know that with a short stroll, you can at least get a can of beans or some red licorice, and that if you have no money, the storekeeper might let you run a tab if he or she knows you. (One morning I saw a lady wearing her pyjamas buying a muffin and the newspaper; she didn't mind if the storekeeper saw her in her pyjamas—it was as if it was her kitchen, her own home.)

The other element that gives corner stores such charm is that they are usually small and rather cozy, and this makes them different from the local convenience store. The corner store is also convenient, but that's not its main goal; the corner store's main goal is to be part of the community. Convenience stores focus on fast food, tabloid magazines with anorexic starlets on their covers, and lotto tickets—not very community oriented—and the light is usually a glaring fluorescent and the floor is a dirty beige lino-leum, and outside there is a sticky waste can and a chewing gum-laden asphalt entrance. But the corner store is spotless—the owner sweeps the sidewalk, hangs up a flower basket, and proudly displays the good things in life—flowers, soap, local greeting cards, and unique sweets.

Corner stores often cater to the single person who may be elderly and living alone nearby and may need only one potato, not a bag. Some older people make it part of their daily routine to shop for dinner, and a chat with the proprietor a little ways down the street fills their day immensely; for many, their daily shop plus a stroll to the duck pond *is* their day. Suffice it to say that the corner store is one feature of a neighbourhood that holds a community together.

Continuing along the street toward the harbour, you come upon the very environmentally conscious Union of British Columbia Municipalities building. In the spring, a subtle sweet smell from a magnificent white plum tree wafts up the sidewalk to greet you. The property has a working rain garden, one of the first in Victoria. A rain garden is a way of filtering and conserving runoff water from the rain. Water is directed from the roof garden (which also serves as habitat and food source for birds and insects as well as regulating warmth and coolness indoors) and the gutters into a rock pit and plant garden. The water is then filtered through the rocks and roots and used for irrigation, stored, or drained off into our stormwater system as clean water, which is good, as it eventually ends up in the ocean.

The building is fascinating indoors and out, and you may take an informative, self-guided tour and learn about the numerous environmental elements, which include the furniture and interior design. Here are some highlights: the rebar in the construction was ninety-eight percent recycled metal, and the boardroom chairs are of one hundred percent recycled material; the stairwell is composed of concrete mixed with locally recycled glass, and the beams were milled from pine-beetle-killed wood from the interior of British Columbia. "Beetlecrete" is a concrete containing woodchips from the milled pine-beetle wood, and it was used for the countertops. And rather than linoleum, a flooring called "marmoleum" was used, which is made largely of linseed oil and wood flour. The windows open for fresh air (ironically, just like the heritage hotel up the street).

I have nothing but praise for those who are "going green" and recycling everything, but I think it's funny that Gran used to open windows because there weren't air conditioners then, and that she used to boil eggshells for calcium during the war, and that Russian peasants and other downtrodden poor people had to recycle all the wood they could find for warmth during the harsh winters, and that farmers piped the methane from their livestock sheds and barns to heat water, and it all cost nothing. Now, to go green costs twice as much. And think of how people had to reuse and recycle during the Great Depression! Even the doll's house at the Art Gallery of Greater Victoria, a real work of intricate craftsmanship, was made of mahogany remnants that came from an old church organ.

Really, all we have done is taken the old logical ideas from the past and made them modern, and put a bureaucratic gold seal on them, a stamp of standard approval from an environmental consultant. I am indeed glad we know not to waste after a few decades of *great* waste. Gran used to throw grey water from the kitchen sink or her bath outside onto the plants with galvanized pails—now we have rain gardens and pumps and gizmos and filters, and we are warned that the grey water might poison us if we put it on vegetables. It's an attitude similar to airport security, fearing that we could blow up a plane with a tube of toothpaste! But as I said, I'm glad we are going *back* to sensibility (even though the builders and politicians think we are moving forward).

Across the street from the UBCM building is the Queen's Printer, which was originally established in 1859 in one of the Birdcages, the small square buildings with the elegant swooping roofs that handled the government business of the new colony of Vancouver Island. The Birdcages were on the same site as the present-day Parliament Buildings—they were our original capital buildings. In fact, this area is called Birdcage Walk. The Birdcages were so cold in winter that the ink froze in the pots and government business often had to be delayed until the ink melted.

The printing and binding of political and official documents was first done on a little hand press that was shipped over from London. The first man hired as the Queen's Printer was Captain E. Hammond King. Captain King printed the colony's government documents and publications for Great Britain, for Queen Victoria. As government grew, so did the business of printing. Today, the Queen's Printer is alive and well and is composed of many departments, which copy, edit, print, and record all our government goings-on.

In the late 1800s, Francis Rattenbury won the competition to design the new Parliament Buildings, and they are magnificent—the numerous green copper domes actually look to me more like birdcages than the little originals.

You can take a free, self-guided tour (the wooden front doors open at 8:30) or a tour with a guide, and there is also a lovely self-guided tour you can take around the grounds. Inside, it is well worth the visit to see the ceiling murals of our four original industries—agriculture, fishing, logging, and mining; stained-glass windows inlaid with local jade; plaster and gold-leaf reliefs, Italian marble decor, historic photographs, and the wonderful, eight-sided rotunda. Rattenbury designed the rotunda with eight sides to be different from

Parliament Buildings at Night

the American rotundas, which were round—a very forward-thinking decision.

You can also learn about the mace, and the difference between *our* lion, on the British Columbia coat of arms, and the lion on the British coat of arms (and why they are different). You can also learn about our official tartan; the white in our tartan represents the dogwood, our provincial flower, the green is for the forests, the red for the maple leaf, blue for the ocean, and gold for the sun and crown. (It's almost like the Hudson's Bay Company blankets—apparently the yellow stripe is for the harvest, the green is for the trees, and the red is for the blood shed when fighting for Canada—a man in the kitchen department of the Bay told me this.)

Outside, the Parliament Buildings are just as spectacular. A little brochure I picked up says that Rattenbury loved to showcase local materials and therefore constructed the buildings from "rough-hewn Haddington Island stone . . . Nelson Island granite . . . and Jervis Inlet slate . . ." Gosh, this Mr. Rattenbury truly was ahead of his time, or was he? Maybe our society just forgot for a while to "buy local." A local postcard states that the Parliament Building roofs cover an area of over six acres! Francis Rattenbury had a gruesome end to his life—he was murdered with a mallet by his second wife's boyfriend, and after the murder she committed suicide—a real-life Greek tragedy.

There are numerous free brochures and fact sheets to collect in the lobby (including a description of Rattenbury's fate); you can read about British Columbia's first women politicians, or how the provincial budget process works. And there's even a little gift shop selling trinkets such as "Parli-Mints." I am almost ashamed of saying that one of the best parts about museums, galleries, and historic sites are the gift shops. It's as if I need to buy something to cling to the memory of the site and the experience.

On a sunny day, with the white boats bobbing in the harbour across the road, it's truly a treat to stroll the grounds and see the landmarks on the Parliament Buildings, which are as interesting and as elegant as the interior. At the back of the library wing, for example, are two features worth noting: the Centennial Fountain, which depicts four bronze animals symbolizing our geography and First Nations cultures, and a large plaque in a cairn with bronze reliefs of famous explorers and politicians, placed to correspond with their sandstone statues high on the building's corners and balconies. It includes Sir Francis Drake, Sir James Douglas, Simon Fraser, and Alexander Mackenzie. There are female statues as well, representing the arts of painting, music, sculpture, and architecture, but they are not on the plaque—maybe they should have their own plaque!

The sunken rose garden on the west side is where one of the historic Birdcages once stood (that's why it is sunken). In the front, on the expansive lawn, are commemorative trees, fountains, statues, and a thick, stolid totem pole. The pole is called the Knowledge Pole, and it is topped by a loon—the teacher, which symbolizes Aboriginal traditions; under the loon is the fisherman, and under him is the bone player, playing a game with all people who do not share the same spoken language; and finally the grand frog that comes from an ancient mountain story.

The frog is very symbolic for First Nations people, and in a totem, it may be hidden in a figure's ear or belly button. Some clans believe that the frog is a symbol of wealth (which takes its form in copper), and other clans believe that Frog can call them back from the dead. Totem pole symbols are fascinating. A face that is upside down might indicate a punishment or insult toward a clan member; some symbols are simply whimsical, but most have deep meanings. One of the tallest totem poles in the world is in Beacon Hill Park near Dallas Road. It was erected in 1956 and is 127 feet 7 inches high.

On the very top of the Parliament Buildings, gleaming like a Greek god, straight and regal, stands a proud, golden Captain Vancouver. From my aquafit class in the Grand Pacific Hotel, I can see him glinting in the sun through a slit in the skylight above the pool—me half-heartedly doing leg kicks in waist-high ozonated water, possibly but not likely increasing my heart rate by a beat or two, while glancing at Captain Vancouver, who crossed the stormy seas and charted our waters, overcoming disease, loneliness, exhaustion, and stresses too hard to even imagine.

The Royal BC Museum is spectacular, and there a few things worth noting outside it. If you walk around the outer courtyard you will see a beautiful piece of public art—it's a bronze sculpture of a family, smooth and polished, by the famous Canadian printmaker and sculptor Jack Harman. Jack hailed from Gibsons on the Sunshine Coast, where he established his foundry in 1962, the first sculpture foundry in BC. His beautiful works in polished bronze can be seen all across Canada and include a sculpture of Queen Elizabeth on horseback at the Parliament Buildings in Ottawa. Jack died in 2001 at age seventy-four. I love the sculpture of the family beside our museum and get a little thrill every time I see it—it's a great piece of public art that I think may go largely unnoticed because of its streetside location, tucked behind a damp garden of native ferns under a pine tree.

The British Columbia Archives is in the lower section of the museum, and if you take the steps down from the street, you will come upon a beautiful pond and native-plant garden, and a bench on which to sit and reflect in the cool shade of the flowering red currants. A distinctive sculpture by another famous Canadian artist, Elza

Mayhew (1916–2004), sits quietly in the pond, stretching upward toward the sunlight. Mayhew's distinguished bronze and aluminum sculptures are formed from symmetrical geometric shapes, some tall, some squat, and remind me of little Mayan shrines or temples for worshipping something greater than ourselves. As in a totem pole, you can see the spirituality, even though the symbols are simply lovely shapes that fit together like a piece of architecture. Mayhew has described her sculptures as representing the dignity of the human state, ritualistic and meditative. Her work is in various locations around town—you can't miss it.

Another highlight of this little hive of activity on the corner of Belleville and Government Streets is the Netherlands Centennial Carillon, also known as "the Singing Tower," which sits next to a hot dog and ice cream vendor and a set of dinosaur footprints. Across the street is a statue of Emily Carr, who seems to have enormous feet and a large round head! The carillon is an actual musical instrument, housed in an eighty-nine-foot cement tower in front of the museum. It was a gift from the Dutch community in British Columbia in honour of Canada's centennial year in 1967. Canadians played an important role in liberating Holland in the Second World War, and the Dutch, appreciating this, have remained great friends of ours.

The carillon consists of sixty-two brass bells (cast in the Netherlands), which are struck—they do not swing. The carillonneur, weather permitting (more often in the summer), climbs the seventy-five steps and then a ladder to play songs that waft and echo across the harbour. One bleak and freezing winter day, I was walking along the causeway, the sleet beating across my face, the sailboats bashing against the docks, their bleached ropes stretched and groaning in the wind—everything grey, wet, and windswept—when suddenly, from the dismal freezing mists, there came a muffled ringing of "Hello Dolly." There were perhaps one or two off-key notes, maybe due to the numb fingers of the musician, but it was a humorous addition to a walk on a winter's day along the deserted Inner Harbour. And our Victoria carillonneur is a woman!

Along the street eastward, just a short walk from the carillon, is one of Victoria's lawn-bowling clubs. On a nice day you will see the players in their bright whites carefully strategizing where to roll their balls on the green, impeccably kept lawn surrounded by clean and freshly painted benches.

Records in Britain suggest that lawn bowling was first practised in the thirteenth century, but

The Cridges were strong anti-racists and promoted education of Victoria's children; they had nine children of their own but devoted much of their time to helping local orphans and the poor. Edward Cridge suddenly went blind in his old age and died at ninety-five. The Church of Our Lord, where Reverend Cridge preached, is a National Historic Site and regularly has clever and humorous religious messages displayed; a recent one was "Life is Fragile, Handle With Prayer." They also note that the church initials spell COOL.

When Victoria was settled, this whole area was a mud flat at the head of James Bay. The Inner Harbour (the bay) came up this far and was fed by a stream beyond; the stream is still flowing underground. This area is known as the Humboldt Valley. It is a little area of downtown that isn't a valley per se, but rather a lovely sloping street with richly historical landscaped heritage structures and woodland gardens at the top and fresh, spacious, and clean modern urban design at the lower end.

Alexander von Humboldt was a brilliant and original thinker, explorer, and naturalist who studied everything from the Earth's magnetic fields to orchids in the seventeenth century. Humboldt was Prussian but spent his life travelling extensively through Latin America and later in Russia. He was very good-looking, and his portraits show him dressed in a white scarf similar to the type that Mr. Darcy (Colin Firth) wore in the BBC series

early monarchs outlawed the increasingly popular sport for fear it would distract people from excelling in archery, a skill needed in the many wars between England and France and other countries. The oldest record of a bowling green is the Southampton Old Bowling Green, used in 1299. Many bowling clubs offer help to the visually impaired by stringing lines along the greens to guide the players' aim.

Just past the lawn-bowling club is a charming little corner park with pathways and shade trees amongst fern gardens and lawns. In the centre are some informative signs dedicated to the clergyman Edward Cridge and his wife, Mary. Next door stands the beautiful heritage wooden board-and-batten Church of Our Lord, designed in the style of Carpenter Gothic by the English architect John Teague and built in 1875. Teague was a well-known local architect in early Victoria who also designed City Hall and a few buildings in the naval dockyard; he was also the mayor of Victoria in 1894.

Pride and Prejudice. So respected was Humboldt that many species of plants and animals are named after him—there's the Humboldt squid, Humboldt's hog-nosed skunk, and the *Salix humboldtiana*, a South African willow.

At the top end of the Humboldt Valley is St. Ann's Academy, a highlight of Victoria's heritage sites. The great stone building with the red turret at its peak was the first four-storey building in Victoria. St. Ann's, built between 1871 and 1910, used to be a convent school. The architecture is French, as the four original Sisters were from Quebec. There is something very charming and Canadian about Victoria having such a contribution from French history. I find it another reason to embrace Quebec as being part of Canada—I am proud of Quebec, and I love the fact that it plays such a historic role.

Beyond the tall iron gates at the entrance to St. Ann's is a vast landscape of orchards, woodlands, gardens, and hedgerows. Up the stone steps, the beautifully exhibited history of the Sisters and their lives includes parlours, the Sisters' artwork, schoolrooms, and even the priest's breakfast room.

Not to be missed is the charming little novitiate garden, a private manicured side garden where the younger novice Sisters could go to contemplate nature, pick herbs, or pursue gentle recreational activities. But the most splendid sight of all is the chapel, built in 1858 as Victoria's first Roman

Catholic church and later added to the school. The decorations and ambience of the chapel reflect rural French-Canadian churches—ornate altars, tapestries, marble trimmings and carvings, gold-leaf, stained glass, religious paintings, plaster reliefs and busts, and a 1913 pipe organ. The academy and grounds have been exquisitely restored, the chapel in historic ornate Quebec Baroque style in gold, white, and pale blue.

You can take a self-guided tour of the academy and its grounds; the little booklet is a delight and has some lovely, sensitive quotes from the Sisters and students who once lived and worked there. Information sheets, little prayers, and trinkets are also given out, all in a gentle and modest manner, and there is even a gift shop with T-shirts. The grand academy is now used as government offices, but the building is worth the visit and the grounds make for a pleasant stroll with interpretive signage throughout.

From the high stone steps of the academy amongst the apple trees, you can see another architectural heritage treasure, St. Joseph's Hospital, across the road, also associated with St. Ann's Academy (some Sisters were nurses). As with St. Ann's, the massive, solid building has a red turret reaching for heaven on its rooftop. St. Joseph's also

Beehives at Fairmont Empress Hotel

has mature shrubs and trees and its own chapel. It was a hospital but is now in private hands and is used as housing, with many of its heritage features preserved. It was at St. Joseph's that Emily Carr's sister, Elizabeth, was nursed during her final days, suffering from breast cancer, and so, in appreciation for the Sisters' compassionate care, Emily gave them a lovely painting titled *Wild Lilies*. *Wild Lilies* is beautiful; I like it as much as the shafts of light that fall between the swirling giant cedars in her later work, the subject that made Emily famous.

The Sisters have, in turn, kindly donated the valuable work to the Art Gallery of Greater Victoria, as well as other art they have collected over the years. In 2012, the Sisters donated a vast collection to the Royal BC Museum. Many of their artifacts date back to 1857 and include hand-carved rosary beads and an 1858 Bible. The Sisters' original little schoolhouse also sits in the peaceful garden beside the museum, amongst the flowering plum trees and an impressive collection of totem poles.

Around the corner from St. Joseph's is Mount St. Mary Hospital, also at one time associated with the Sisters of St. Ann. Mount St. Mary in the past was a hospital for extended care but is now a modern facility for "complex care." I met someone who said that Mount St. Mary is the most compassionate hospital her old father has ever known; he wanted rice pudding with raisins like his mum used to make, so the nurse made it for him using her mother's recipe. Now that's a great nurse!

Down the hill from the historic and shaded landscapes of the Sisters is a modern array of gleaming, turquoise glass towers surrounded by fountains and white patios. The lower part of the Humboldt Valley is made up of plastic-surgery and liposuction clinics, spas, and little cafés serving chilled glasses of crisp French white wine with appallingly smelly cheeses (which are delicious!), along with the two very chic Winchester art galleries.

The galleries are set back behind a clean concrete patio, which serves as a place to sip espressos amongst some colourful and interesting outdoor sculpture: another Elza Mayhew (made of solid aluminum) and two large steel structures, one bright red and the other bright blue, titled *Music One* and *Music Two*. There are other modern pieces strategically placed—one looks like a combination of a rain barrel and beer keg that has rolled in from the

street. It's an extremely important piece of art by our well-known Victoria artist Mowry Baden, and it is titled *Toy Amenity Satellite*.

My own taste in art is very traditional—I am never sure what I am supposed to think when I see modern or minimalist art. There was a painting at the Victoria art gallery that was simply a canvas painted bright pink. There it hung on a white wall, just this pink square. The ironic thing was that it said nothing, but it consumed me. The reaction was philosophical—I seemed to have been doing

Mount St. Mary Hospital

more thinking than the artist and I remember feeling that this just was not fair—How Dare He! And then I became mad at myself for being taken in by a pink square. In retrospect, I think that my reaction wasn't minimalist, even though the visual piece of art was. But I may have had the final word because if it was really minimalist, why did the artist even need colour? Sometimes just loving a painting of wild lilies for its beauty is what it's all about—it's much less stressful and as I age, I just don't have the energy to mentally argue with a painting of a pink square.

The patio in front of these galleries is worth noting. Sunken slightly from the sidewalk, the smooth white concrete becomes a curving stream not only amongst the modern art, but between small fountains and pools, and blocks of shrubbery. Sculptured fish embedded in the "creek" follow your movement. The design of this fake waterway is beautiful and calming; it is perhaps even lovelier than some real creeks and ponds and scraggly shrubbery. Isn't it interesting that something that substitutes for nature can actually be as lovely or lovelier? To a nature lover like me, this was an epiphany!

The grand, palace-like, ivy-covered Fairmont Empress Hotel, also designed by Francis Rattenbury (the architect of the Parliament Buildings), stands at the base of Humboldt Street. The Empress was originally a Canadian Pacific Railway hotel (there's one in every province) and is known for its extravagant afternoon English teas, posh interior, and delicious dinners at the (East) Indian buffet in the Bengal Room, but perhaps many people do not know that the Empress also is home to eight hundred thousand Carniolan and Italian honey bees, which produce the delicious honey that is featured in the Empress's restaurant menus and teas. The bees, cared for by a professional beekeeper, live in ten hives in the Centennial Garden and pollinate the fragrant flowered landscapes and rose beds of the hotel. Over one thousand pounds of honey can be produced in a year. Victoria is known as "the city of gardens," which makes it a delight for the bees.

Some residents in our neighbourhood actually have their own hives in their back gardens. The life cycle and lifestyle of the bee is one of the most amazing on earth. I have always wondered how the queen bee is chosen by the others to be the queen; a friend of mine thinks it is because she's "at the right place at the right time" but I think it is more that she exhibits the sort of leadership charisma that the other bees just resign themselves to following. I went to high school with girls like that. Whatever the reason it takes to become the queen, we love and need our bees, and May 29 is the official Day of the Honey Bee.

The Empress is also known as the place a poor frightened cougar hid out a few years ago, lost and

disoriented in the lower car park. I cannot recall how the story ended; I am sure that if it was possible to catch the cougar and take him back to the nearby woods, the City would have done that. Cougars are also called mountain lions and they are plentiful in the region, along with black bears. Cougars kill and eat deer—one deer will last one about a week. Their jaws are for slicing, not chewing, so they have great difficulty eating (chewing) frozen carcasses. Good thing for the cougar that it rarely freezes here.

On the front lawn of the Empress stands a healthy, multi-stemmed arbutus tree. *Arbutus* is from the Latin meaning "strawberry tree" and it is the only broad-leafed evergreen tree native to Canada. The Pacific coast here is its northernmost habitat but it is found quite far south and was first recognized in 1749 by a Spanish missionary in California. The arbutus is a striking tree with its peeling deep-red outer bark and hard, cool, green inner trunk. The tree, because of the structure of its white flowers (followed by red berries) belongs to the heather family.

It is said that the First Nations used the arbutus wood to make board games, and boiled the leaves, bark, and roots to make a potion for curing colds and flu. It sounds as if that might be a bitter mixture but maybe it's better than what some of the drug companies put out these days. They warn you on television in a rapid verbal spew of a dozen frightening side effects such as passing out, vomiting, blindness, impotence, dizziness, constipation, and suicidal tendencies—they advise that you see your doctor immediately if you have these side effects. I think I'd rather have the flu.

Across the road from the Empress is the causeway overlooking the Inner Harbour. On a sunny day, the upper and lower causeways are bustling with tourists, red double-decker buses, buskers, and street vendors. The harbour is always a hive of activity, full of seaplanes, expensive yachts and sailboats, whale-watching boats, fishboats, kayaks and little harbour ferries. Sometimes there are near collisions, with all the congestion. One year I was the drummer on a dragon boat in a race, and during the warm-up I sort of steered us into ramming Merv Griffin's great white luxury cruiser, and then when we backed up, we hit the Undersea Gardens!

The buskers range from magicians to musicians to mimes to acrobats on stilts. Most of the vendors are First Nations craftspeople who make traditional wares such as the famous knitted Cowichan slippers, mittens, and socks. They usually sit patiently along the grassy knoll in front of the pink daisies that spell out "Welcome To Victoria" and work on their crafts, oblivious to the old grey-and-red *Coho* docking or bellowing its hollow horn as it slowly makes its way out of the harbour, or the hooting of the bright, slick, red-and-blue *Clipper*, a fast catamaran that glides down scenic Puget Sound to Seattle every day.

The First Nations craftspeople are very friendly and love telling you their traditional cultural histories. I spoke to a modest quiet woman who made dream catchers and beaded jewellery. She told me she was a Mi'kmaq from Prince Edward Island. Her dream catchers were simple and pretty: a circle of hemp twine woven like a spider's web with some local semi-precious stones such as the amber tiger's eye, the opaque green jade, or the pale pinkish-grey rhodonite. Each stone symbolized something special, such as courage or luck. Below the web were elegant feathers; the legend is that when you dream at night, your bad and evil thoughts will get trapped in the web, but your good and positive dreams will filter through the web and down through the feathers and come true for you when you wake up. She also made little dream catchers that you can hang in your car—wouldn't it be wonderful if it were all true!

I also spoke to Eric, a local First Nations man who sits on the lower causeway every day of the year, rain or shine (if it is raining he sits under his large red umbrella) and carves symbolic animals. His uncle taught him how to carve, with the little sharp tools with wooden handles, and Eric is passing the skill on to his younger cousin. Eric likes to use red cedar but his uncle uses pine. "People like to hear a story," he told me. "So I tell them that the hummingbird is the symbol of joy and friendship." He leaned over with great concentration, and finely and patiently eased his chisel along the outstretched fluttering wing of the little bird lying on his lap.

What the Carver Knows
Janet Rogers

he sits on sidewalks
sizing up passers-by
clutching his curved knife
drawing deep confident gouges
transforming yellow cedar

"Bear?" he's asked
"Beaver," he explains

and waits for change
we all wait for change
says, he's been to church, yesterday
they pray for him there
"Worth more than money.
Thank God, it stopped raining."

two bucks, he thinks is a lot
drinks decaf between wood shavings
red pride has not abandoned him
resides inside, quiet like heart-felt
memories
a childhood, good and cared for
a family strong and revered
he is here

he claims the cement as home
on a damp street corner
in a city which sees so many like him
it rolls its eyes as numbers grow
he moans and bleeds
lets droplets fall
onto a thirsty earth
seeping down to meet
the bones of those who've gone
before

we live envious
of his skills and ability to survive
while we complain daily

of superficial hardships
and spoiled-rotten heart-aches

the beaver bites back
the carver smiles sideways
the rain begins again
while we run for cover

There are all sorts of little extra things to see and to read about on the causeway—the original old street gas lamp, a gift from Britain; the Loyalist Rose bushes, named after the United Empire Loyalists; and one of the seven giant, beautifully crafted spindle whorls that sit at various locations in Victoria, symbolizing the original First Nations villages and hunting grounds. These whorls were used in First Nations weaving. The whorls are lovely, elegant works of public art with a strong and moving meaning behind them; they signify special places in the land of the Lekwungen (known today as the Esquimalt and Songhees Nations). The Native name for each location translates as a description, such as "Place Of Mud," the lower causeway, which was originally muddy, albeit rich in shellfish; "Warmed By The Sun," the sunny slope in Beacon Hill Park facing the sea; and "Bitter Cherry," the area downtown next to City Hall.

You can read all about the various First Nations locations in a beautifully illustrated pamphlet called *Signs of Lekwungen*, available at various shops and public facilities around town such as City Hall or the Royal BC Museum gift shop.

Of course I have to mention again my hero Captain Cook, who stands handsomely on the upper causeway across from the Empress. George Vancouver got the glitter and the elevation overlooking us all, but Cook stands on the harbour with us. Actually, Vancouver was a midshipman on Cook's voyage to Nootka, the area where Cook anchored when he visited the west coast of Vancouver Island. Vancouver returned later on a much more detailed charting of our local waters.

Behind the lovely statue of Captain Cook is a series of small brass plaques, each dedicated to a historic ship that graced our harbour during Victoria's development. And farther along, on the corner, is a pretty peace garden. It's amazing what you see when you stop and really observe the surroundings—a plaque which describes a shipwreck, a waffle maker, the skyline or the enlarged historic photos of the harbour bathers that cover the Hydro boxes.

Beyond lower Government Street, people can amble through the quaint, historic downtown area, which is full of busy little shops selling everything from British Columbia jade to English tea to Irish linens to Cuban cigars. British Columbia produces half of the world's supply of jade, mined in the interior and up north. You can watch an informative video at the jade shop that shows the jade in

Captain Cook

The social history of Cook's life, both on and off the oceans, makes for very interesting reading, especially excerpts from his and Vancouver's personal journals as well as notes from their crews. Cook is regarded as the first British man to touch our island's soil.

Cook wrote kindly about the Native people and noted that the Spanish must have been here first because of the type of silver spoons the Natives had, which they used as necklaces!

Many people do not realize that the multi-talented Cook had charted Canada's east coast on a previous voyage, including the Gulf of St. Lawrence and Newfoundland, and he did it all patiently with a lead line, measuring the depths, the topography of the sea floor, and the currents. His early training proved valuable—he had worked for years on the coal ships that travelled from Britain across the frigid and wild North Sea and through the fjords of Scandinavia.

Our hero Captain Cook is also known for the care he took of his crew. Cook realized that scurvy was not a disease, but an affliction caused by the lack of vitamins found in vegetables and fruit, so he devised a menu of sauerkraut, brewers' malt, and "marmalade of carrots" and even brewed a spruce beer at Nootka! Also, every man was given a ration of twenty pounds of onions,

picked up en route. At Nootka, Cook and his men found wild garlic, nettles, and wild raspberries. Men were flogged if they did not eat what Cook provided.

Some of the men who accompanied Cook on his voyages had enviable jobs. To record pictorial details, there was the expedition artist, a bit like the war artists who went to war to paint the scenes of history on the battlefield. To study and translate new languages, there was a naturalist/doctor; Cook used the word wakashan, which means "friendship," often in his personal journals.

There was also the ship's surgeon, and the ship's botanist. George Vancouver's botanist was Archibald Menzies. Menzies collected cuttings, plants, and seeds from all over the world, studied them, and illustrated his journals with beautiful sketches and descriptions.

Punishment on the voyages was harsh, and took the form of lashing. A man would receive twenty-four lashes for insolence on Vancouver's ship.

Cook's surgeon, Dr. Samwell, wrote the following about Cook: "Unrivalled and alone, on him all eyes turned; he was our leading star . . . He always kept a good table . . . Was rather bashful . . . His person was above six feet high . . . his head was small . . . his nose exceedingly well shaped."

the glacial veins of the mountains, and the six-foot saw used to slice this lovely green stone. Jade is very hard, so diamond-tip drills have to be used to remove it from the rock. In the 1500s, the Spanish believed that jade would cure ailments in the kidneys so they called the mineral the "loinstone."

There are ice cream stands and bookshops and pubs. You can buy chocolates, maple candy, hemp clothing, homemade soaps, and glass art (there were some fabulous, delicious-looking, pink, hand-blown-glass cupcakes in one gallery window). Souvenir shops sell beautiful First Nations postcards, smoked salmon, and Cowichan sweaters. I also need to mention Munro's Books, one of the grandest Canadian bookshops, located in an equally grand heritage building.

The sidewalks are lined with carefully pruned trees with ornate iron plates around their bases. At night, the trees are lit with little white lights, and the Parliament Buildings are also trimmed with bulbs that are reflected in the harbour—the place looks like a glittering and magical fairyland. It's absolutely beautiful—nothing is overdone and there is no obvious neon—there's something to be said for taste.

Some of the sidewalk surfaces are made up of little squares of purple glass. These purple-glassed sidewalks are of great heritage value, for underneath them is a maze of tunnels strengthened by posts and beams. The passageways were used for

coal and supply storage by the local merchants in the early 1900s. The tunnels were lit by the prisms on the underside of the glass blocks, and over time the prisms of glass turned wonderful shades of pink and purple due to the manganese content in the glass when it oxidized with the sunlight. On a sunny day, there must have been moments of beauty in the dim underworld beneath the city.

There are not many purple-glass sidewalks left. One is on the corner of Broughton and Broad Streets. These sidewalks may be preserved by the City of Victoria—there is talk about restoring them

Government Street

and adding illumination from below—wouldn't that be a magnificent nocturnal sight above?!

Just a couple of blocks up from the water are more shops, and larger and newer office and government buildings. Up the hill is the Victoria courthouse, as well as the grand grey-stone Christ Church Cathedral, and beside it historic Pioneer Square, the oldest cemetery in Victoria, operating between 1855 and 1873. Pioneer Square is a cool, shady, and gentle place to sit and have a little think and is well worth a visit and walkabout.

The cemetery is undergoing a restoration—old tombstones and the graves of important historic characters, politicians, and families are being mapped and preserved, and interpretive signage is being added throughout the little park. There are one thousand three hundred people interred at the cemetery, according to a recent newspaper article.

Originally, Fort Victoria had a little graveyard in the location of what is now the corner of Douglas and Johnson Streets, but nearby pigs began to root up the corpses. (That's what pigs do, but they can only root so deep, so I imagine that these were shallow graves.) So Governor James Douglas moved the graveyard to higher ground and farther away from the pigs to what is now Pioneer Square. Prisoners who were held at the jail in the town's Bastion Square had the gruesome task of digging up the human remains and reburying them at the new site.

At the new cemetery, bodies were segregated as to religion and ethnicity; there was a Catholic plot, an Anglican plot (they got a corner for the navy!), a Chinese section, and even a Hawaiian area. Separate sites for religions and ethnic backgrounds—how strange it is that even in death, we cannot rest in peace *together*, even the navy. When the gold rush hit Victoria, the population increased massively and the graveyard had to be moved to Ross Bay.

There's a mind-boggling technological method of mapping burial sites called "ground-penetrating radar." On a grid, the area is scanned with echoes that reflect back as electromagnetic pulses; the archaeologist patiently walks across the area with a high-tech gizmo that measures changes in soil density, i.e., graves.

Informative maps and illustrations can be seen in a lovely little book I came across called *Victoria Underfoot—Excavating a City's Secrets*. The local Old Cemeteries Society has also published a fascinating brochure listing famous characters who are buried at Pioneer Square; it describes who they were and how they died. For example, here's an excerpt: "Wallace Obelisk. Here lie Kate Wallace and three of her children. She was the daughter of Hudson's Bay Company chief factor, John Work. Her marriage to Charles Wentworth Wallace was unhappy partly because he squandered their money. After they had to sell their home in 1869 Kate died of consumption."

Oh those cruel old diseases! Gran used to talk about her friend dying of quinsy. Things are so much better now, physically at least.

Christ Church Cathedral used to be where the courthouse is now. I have never been to court (except when I witnessed a horse theft on a remote island a long time ago) and the judicial system has always held fascination for me, a combination of drama and justice and emotional suspense. I asked my friend Jane Henderson, QC, to fill me in on justice in Victoria. She works with divorce and separation issues, so what better person to ask about suspense and fairness? And she even offered to give me a tour of the courthouse.

Jane became a lawyer years ago. I remember Mum talking on the phone to Jane's mother, Barbara (my godmother); Mum was really excited because Jane had just won her first case. She was defending an old farmer who had bought a milking cow thinking it was "with calf" (pregnant) but it wasn't, and the settlement was that the farmer was given his money back *plus* he kept the cow!

Jane and I had lunch first at a little Tibetan restaurant near the courthouse—I had to make reservations because it is so popular. We had a delicious mixture of deep-fried vegetables and curry, and rice and breads, and a mild cheese with spinach.

We chatted about current legal trends; marriage disputes are often mediated rather than going to court, and the growing trend now is arbitration.

It's a destructive and sad thing (but I understand it—the emotional upheavals) when revenge and hurt and anger get in the way of common sense and logic at the end of a marriage. A sensitive and patient mediator would be a godsend—what a skill to have, and how good it is for society to resolve a dispute without animosity.

After lunch we strolled up to the courthouse, a tall, square, beige and yellow building with cement steps and rows of plain, rectangular windows. The building really looks as if it could do with a new coat of paint; it looks tired and a bit sooty, as if it belongs in a Minsk suburb.

When Jane and I were walking up the steps, an energetic little man in a red jacket and pin-striped pants bounded up beside us—he looked familiar. Jane smiled at him and said, "Good afternoon, Your Honour." Then she whispered to me his name and said that he was a very important judge, and that the judges in the courthouse even have their own elevator! But it was great that they also come and go through the main entrance like everyone else.

Inside there was a great, dimly lit hallway, crowded with people paying fines at glassed-in counters, or sitting around waiting for something. Jane gave me a grand tour, starting upstairs in the library, a small area crammed with worn, leather-bound books of law; she found one on a back shelf that she had scrawled in forty years ago when she was a law student.

Christ Church Cathedral

Then we went into a courtroom. There were two big, burly, tattooed men (Jane whispered, "The accused") with shaved heads and pudgy necks sitting behind a Plexiglas shield ("in case someone wanted to shoot them," she whispered again) surrounded by tired-looking sheriffs with ear pieces (and I think one had a gun). These were real criminals! It was exciting but tense. Jane said that the judges and clerks have secret alarm buzzers to press if things get violent. Well, after five minutes of listening to a little lawyer in his great black robe making a case full of legal jargon about a lack of evidence, we crept out.

Downstairs was the small-claims court, where a poor electrician was being sued by a couple who refused to pay him because of some misunderstanding over the extra cost of some kitchen counters in their new basement suite. Nothing had been put in writing and it was revealed that no building permits had been obtained but the judge told the couple that they had to pay the man. He also told them off for not having building permits, and right in the middle of his reaming out the electrician for not having a contract, the courtroom went dark and the computers all groaned to a halt—the power had gone out! It turned out that the power was out all over town because of a lightning strike.

That was my tour of the courthouse, a place of mystery and intrigue, of secrets and bad behaviour, drama, suspense, and crime, all combined with high legal intelligence and enormous respect for truth, fairness, and justice. It's a mixture of the worst of the worst and the most dignified system of the land. I don't know which I find more intriguing, the criminals or the judges.

The City has published some very interesting and informative walking-tour brochures, complete with historic photographs; you can find these brochures in the racks on the bottom floor of the mall (the Bay Centre), just beside the escalators. The pamphlets describe various heritage strolls through the downtown streets amongst the many restored historic buildings. The Chinatown stroll is especially intriguing; the map guides you through Fan Tan Alley, named after the gambling game Fan Tan and dubbed "Canada's narrowest street." The Chinese temple is exceptional—up fifty-two steps above a Chinese grocery store is a little room smelling of incense and crowded with gold-and-red prayer altars, statues, offerings of fruit, lanterns, and decorations.

If you would like to learn about the colourful history of Victoria, pick up these well-researched pamphlets, walk through the streets, and read about murders, unlawfulness, gold seekers, high finance in the 1800s, opium dens, haunted hotels, and other spooky places and events.

Fernwood Road at Gladstone

CHAPTER FIVE

Fernwood

The village centre of historic Fernwood, with its surrounding heritage homes, is *the* quintessential, quaint, charming, small neighbourhood. Unlike Cook Street Village and other central neighbourhood meeting places, Fernwood's centre sits on the classic four corners—quirky corners full of diverse culture and activity, smack in the middle of one of the oldest parts of Victoria.

It doesn't take even a minute to realize that you are in an artistic hub when you stand in front of the Belfry Theatre, a renovated nineteenth-century church. Art banners fly from the colourfully painted telephone poles and young artists make their way across the road toward the little galleries, carrying canvases wrapped in brown paper under their arms, or gather at the corner coffee shop to chat or maybe even to philosophize as in the Parisian cafés in the 1920s. There is usually somebody doing something eccentric in the courtyard.

One day, there was an elderly man with a long grey beard, dressed in denim overalls and a purple cape, blowing huge bubbles, which drifted up toward the steeple of the historic Belfry Theatre, from a great grey plastic sword that he dipped into a galvanized pail of soapy water. Now there's a juxtaposition! A sword and bubbles—aha! I get it. That was his art form—a sword and a bubble—a volatile instrument of death and killing, producing a fragile, gentle, floating bubble that wafts up the street. I suppose you could also say that the act of blowing bubbles, plus the bubbles themselves, was a form of public art, and when the bubbles burst, well, who says art has to last forever? This then could provoke the whole philosophical debate of what is time, and how important is it? All this from an eccentric man blowing bubbles on the street. He also had a purple sparkly troll or wizard sort of doll in one pocket, and a worn copy of a book on goblins in the other.

Everyone was kind to him, as if he was a fixture in the neighbourhood, and perhaps that is one way to look at a neighbourhood, to see how their local eccentrics are accepted and treated and embraced. We live in a crazy world with lots of problems, but I like to think that our tolerance for people who are different is improving, and that we are more empathetic toward the bullied ones who march to a different drummer. I think, in Fernwood anyway, that we are in a more compassionate world.

One evening I dropped in to the Fernwood Inn. I sat in the back room in a cozy booth with a glass of wine and admired the beautiful wildlife photographs, framed in rustic wooden frames, hanging on the yellowed walls. Then an extraordinary event began to take place all around me. First, people, mostly older and alone, very nicely dressed, began to arrive and set up music stands throughout the room. Then a band appeared on the little wooden stage. Two of the band members were women and one wore a black T-shirt that said, in big, crazy, white letters, THE MIGHTY UKE.

The woman began to strum and sing "I'd Like to Teach the World to Strum" and everyone joined in, accompanied by a rosy-cheeked, smiling man wearing a pink and yellow Hawaiian shirt, who coolly strummed the bass at the back of the stage.

The two women reminded me of an eastern maritime party—they were full of fun and humour and began playing maritime songs such as "Farewell to Nova Scotia" (all we needed was a step dancer!). They belted out the songs with gusto, stomping their feet and playing their ukuleles. And soon the whole room was singing and playing ukuleles as well. I was in the middle of the monthly ukulele strum-a-long hosted by Diamond Tooth Molly & the Mighty Little Uke Band!

They played a wide selection of Canadian songs, from Gordon Lightfoot to Anne Murray. I couldn't believe that you could play such a variety of songs on the ukulele. In the break, some members oiled and polished their ukuleles; others tuned and tightened their strings and asked the woman on the stage to listen for the right sound, while others discussed the date of the next practice at the Legion across town. One lady admired the new leather carrying case that her friend had purchased from an online ukulele store. A smiling, plump man with

ruddy cheeks, wearing big jeans and red suspenders, plucked away at the tiniest ukulele I have ever seen—his thick pink fingers elegantly touched the strings as the little instrument rested on his stomach.

After the break and another couple of tunes, Diamond Tooth Molly belted out to the audience, "Okay, folks, it's time for the Uke Salute!" and everyone energetically held up their ukuleles by their necks. "I'm counting twenty-two tonight," she yelled with delight before launching into "Makin' Love Ukulele Style." (The second time I attended, she counted forty-eight ukes, and the third time, fifty-four.)

On a glorious, sunny, early-spring day I paid a visit to the nearby Fernwood Compost Education Centre on a large city lot on a quiet, dead-end street right behind Victoria High School. It's the oldest high school in western Canada, says the plaque in front of the massive stone steps; the school started out as a log cabin and now the stolid, elegant, massive sand-coloured structure has a French immersion program and many overseas students.

I strolled over to the compost centre from the village, a pleasant walk along a street lined with historic wooden and red-brick heritage homes, with gardens full of blooming snowdrops, and delicate yellow winter jasmines leaning against porches in need of a paint job after a cold winter.

The compost centre was a little oasis of fertility. There were lush beds of green winter vegetables, a composting toilet, a grey water collection and filtration system with bathtubs (stage three was made up of marsh plants which filter out pollutants), a "green roof" full of budding stonecrop, a native forest garden, and piles of rich organic "black gold," compost created from local kitchen scraps, fallen leaves, and garden waste. My hostess at the compost centre quoted the definition of a native plant from the Native Plant Society of British Columbia as "a plant that occurs naturally in a particular region, ecosystem or habitat—and occurred *prior to European contact*. Native plants can be mosses, ferns, grasses, wildflowers, shrubs, trees and more."

There was a bee area where all the bees were resting for the winter. The compost centre works with mason bees, a native bee that is a good pollinator and will rarely sting you—they look like large black flies and live in tight little cavities that the compost centre provides for them. My host told me that honey is the only food on earth that will keep and will never spoil. Honey in ancient clay vases has been excavated from the tombs in Egypt and is still edible.

From a warm little cabin, the compost centre sells heirloom vegetable seeds, kitchen compost buckets, and all sorts of interesting books and gadgets, and they are more than happy to give you a tour and explain the difference between native plants, noxious weeds, and invasives. But by far the most amazing feature is the straw-bale, natural-plaster-domed cottage and the incredible organic and permacultural worm project going on inside. The sturdy, light grey structure looks like a home for goblins and trolls (anything egg-shaped and oval seems to me to have something to do with trolls!). Inside, a soft and earthy odour comes from underneath the wooden benches that surround the round room. The benches are full of various stages of rich black earth and compost, which house hundreds of very happy earthworms, essential in gardens to break down soils and add further fertility. The wonderful, warm smell of earth comes from the heat and activity within the composted soil. What is it about the warm and humid smell of earth that is so comforting—could it be a subconscious connection to the ground of Mother Earth?

Sandra, a volunteer and permaculture expert, loves and values her worms and demonstrated "worm migration" by coaxing the worms to shift their location with new fresh, rich compost.

The compost centre has a hotline: 386-WORM.

Just a block or two down the street from the compost centre is another beautified city lot named Spring Ridge Commons. The colourful sign tells us that the commons is a permacultural food garden, and that a public common garden means its products are free for anyone to harvest. The garden is a mass of fruit trees and garden beds separated by gravel pathways. The site is the location of an abundant freshwater spring that began to supply Victoria in 1843. The water was first carried to town in barrels by horse cart, but later pumped in through wooden pipes. One of the original wooden pipes sits as a historic monument beside the Selkirk Trestle, which crosses the Gorge waterway downtown.

When water was transported to town from Elk and Beaver Lakes years later, the meadows around the spring in Fernwood were used as municipal yards, and gravel was excavated as fill for other parts of town (the area under the Empress Hotel, for example).

The other historic feature of Spring Ridge Commons is, according to a weathered brass plaque amongst the tangle of campions and marigolds, that it was also the site of a one-room schoolhouse built in 1887. The principal was Isla Tuck, who was well loved and cared so much for her young students that she regularly took them to town and bought them shoes. The school closed in 1957.

One evening in the Fernwood Village, I ventured into a tiny, sweet-smelling café, the Darband Tea House and Hookah Lounge, which advertised Persian teas and Turkish coffees. When you open the red door, you go down some steps and into a tiny, warm, glowing area full of red cushions and orange drapes and rich carpets. The place smelled nice, a combination of sweet and smoke. People were lounging around on the cushions, engaging in a sort of social activity that involved sucking on a tube attached to a tall, elegant, glass-and-brass contraption called a hookah. After some research, I discovered that the hookah is actually an Indian device used for smoking in which the tobacco (or other substances such as sugar-beet sugar) is watered down inside the glass part of the elaborate contraption. It's all completely legal, but not exactly on my list or awareness of urban activities. We couldn't stay that evening when we discovered the little golden hideaway because there was no room, but I will return to experience the interesting pastime of smoking a hookah and order a

Fernwood Compost Education Centre

Turkish coffee. It all seems as though it might take a toll on the body, and also, it feels a bit naughty, or sort of radical, as if we're having secret political meetings or something and that at any minute the place might be raided by the RCMP.

Right next door to the hookah place is another tiny nook called The Paint Box—I think it might be the smallest art school in town. I have never painted anything in my life (perhaps it is because Mum and Dad are such successful Canadian artists) but have always wondered if I have any aptitude at all in that area, so I signed up to take a watercolour lesson. I showed up at dusk on a drizzly winter's evening. The paving stones in the Fernwood courtyard were shiny wet and the colourful posters advertising a bluegrass band at the coffee shop and an art show by brain-damaged students in the lobby of the little theatre across the road were dripping and peeling off the missile-shaped kiosk in front of the tattoo parlour.

I had to push really hard on the door leading from the wet, dismal night into the tiny warm studio, which was crammed with paints and art supplies, at the bottom of a little set of wooden stairs. The brick walls were almost totally covered in watercolours of still lifes, fabric collages, sketches of nudes,

and pastel country scenes. There was a paint-stained sink with glass jars of paintbrushes. A colour wheel dangled from a hook next to a root-bound spider plant.

There was a long table in the centre of the room with blank paper taped to the surface. My instructor, Emily, a kind and gentle-looking young blonde woman wearing an apron and holding a tray of numerous little paint tubes, welcomed me and we began. She suggested that we begin with a landscape, a sunset, in fact, over a lake, and I immediately thought of the pink and grey sunsets Dad does on the Miramichi River in New Brunswick, with a black fly fisherman in hip waders casting his line into the deep river, a row of dark trees on the riverbank in the distance.

Dad's watercolours are technically perfect and accurate, usually of scenes; Mum's are usually of great vases of flowers, watery and loose—that's their personalities, and I wondered what method I would instinctively be drawn to. I had a hunch that I would be like Mum, free and wet and blurred and soft and dripping. I have never been skilled and technical and clever like Dad; maybe I am too emotional and need to have fewer boundaries—I have been disciplined, but not technically skilled, and

Winter Beach, a painting by Molly Lamb Bobak, the author's mother.

that at times has been frustrating. I am sympathetic to those who are determined but unable to skilfully articulate, and I hope they realize that there are other "free" ways to express oneself and an idea.

So Emily and I chatted about life and art as she pulled a worn postcard of a landscape from a drawer and gently had me draw pencil lines across my paper where the purple sea met the pale yellow sky and where the grey treeline met the black rocks and where the silver, mauve, shimmering sea (or maybe it was a lake) met its golden reflection. Well, so far this was a cakewalk, I thought! However, she kept reminding me to cover the pencil lines. Every time she glanced over at my masterpiece, I sort of "choked" and found myself thinking, "Oh please, just let me be," as a huge water splotch in the treeline washed its way into the orange sky.

"Dab the water with a Kleenex," Emily advised, but I didn't really want to. I liked the wetness and wondered if in nature the sky "watered" into the distant dark hills and sea, but I did what she said and dabbed away the water splotch, which created a lovely murky purple dusk.

I soon found out that Emily is the artist who paints the delightful and whimsical scenes on the Hydro poles throughout Fernwood. Apparently, BC Hydro encourages the painting of its poles in order to beautify the neighbourhood—I found it a strange juxtaposition that Hydro is installing Smart meters (which some people think are dangerous) onto every house in the province but at the same time humouring us by allowing us to paint their poles to decorate our streets. I thought I might ask Emily to paint the pole in front of my house in James Bay: a fish theme, perhaps—gold and silver fish in an azure sea, swimming around the pole and into the hawthorn tree.

Then we dabbed in some bleak black trees, possibly cedars, and as I poked away with my little brush, I asked Emily if she would ever like to have a show, because after all, she had been through the university program and was a trained painter, a visual artist. But, refreshingly, she said, "I just love teaching. I love the social-ness of it. I don't need to have an exhibition—I don't produce enough." Emily was not the classic tormented artist, and I am not sure if you need to be tormented to create a great work anyway. Actually, being distracted by your anguish might deter you from creating something wonderful—it may well be a cliché to assume that a great work must be made during mood swings and a tumultuous "episode." Perhaps if people were in this state of angst all the time, their genius might be created on a day when they were happy—who knows?

Emily and I agreed that a great work can never be predicted. Mum told me that one time she was struggling to paint the vision that was in her head and it just wouldn't come out, and then, with no warning whatsoever, "something just floated by and I caught it," she said. I would think an artist of any type would be very fortunate to capture a feeling at exactly the time it passed by—to be moved and to grab it right at the exact moment. Now that's what an artist strives for, the moment when truth and emotion and capture all come together—it's what keeps a creative soul going. I wonder how many artists have gone through their lives without hitting upon that moment, that unpredictable fluke of energy that Mum caught that one time as it "floated by." I think that's what athletes strive for as well, that moment of perfection.

A thumping vibration came through the walls. "That's the hookah emporium," Emily said. I told her that I was too nervous to smoke a hookah.

My wet painting was almost finished! It was so wet that we had to dry it with a hair dryer. I signed my initials on the bottom and titled my master-piece *Vermillion Sunset*.

Emily said that if I returned, we would do a still life, "which is more difficult," she said, "because the sunset was 'flat' and a still life has more dimensions and light and shadow." My heart leapt. She said that I was to bring in a few favourite objects. "Hmmmm," I thought. A thousand items went through my mind—some white shells from a Barcelona beach, Gran's little brass teapot, a jade-green ceramic box made by a peasant in Belarus, a blown-glass pig from Venice, and my Emily Carr ashtray in the shape of a salmon's mouth (which I inherited from my grandfather). I did think for a moment that perhaps it wouldn't be quite right to paint an object created by another artist—that seems rather odd and even pointless, to create something that has already been created! I think art should come out of something the artist feels, not just sees.

I left the tiny studio with my painting under my arm. The audience from the Belfry Theatre was emptying out through the great arched exit; its elegant steeple and stained-glass windows glowed faintly under a street lamp that shone down into the wet courtyard. The warm light flowed from the hookah place onto the sidewalk next door, but I still didn't go in. Across the road, the audience from the little alternative Theatre Inconnu also drifted onto the dark street, perhaps heading for a late-night drink at the wine bar around the corner.

Theatre Inconnu means "unknown theatre." It's a great name for this little company, which has been performing plays in Victoria since 1978, usually in tiny venues that seat perhaps fewer than fifty people, but then, the intimacy of theatre, of life, is what it's all about.

Clayton Jevne, the theatre's artistic director, and I had a drink (or two) at the Fernwood Inn one evening—we sat on high stools by a window that looked out onto yet another drizzly night, and as the rain hit the glass we talked about not only the *intimacy* of theatre but also its unpredictability. Unpredictability is lacking in traditional theatre, and that's okay—it's nice to know what you are getting. Some people don't like surprises, and even more, some people like to have a good time and see a joyful play with a happy ending, not a depressing one—there are times when we just don't want to see reality and the truth of our vulnerabilities and limitations. Clayton's plays are full of truth and reality and it's often not a pretty sight! But it's a play, and just because at times the themes are perhaps a bit morose or even gruesome (as life can be) doesn't mean you cannot enjoy yourself.

When an artist paints a bleak scene with great skill, a scene that moves you, we call it great art, and especially when

The Belfry Theatre

music brings us to tears, we call it genius, but often when a play depicts something sad or unseemly, we are a bit more uncomfortable—perhaps it is because we are among others in an audience and we cannot either move on or turn it off (as in looking at a painting or listening to music). Our feeling of commitment to being stuck there in our seats distracts us and overcomes the art, the play. Theatre might be one of the few art forms that plays this terrible trick on us—it's like having our mouths

washed out with soap, and yet, perhaps ironically, that makes it a more powerful art form.

Clayton loves plays that "take him by surprise" and that "rip his heart out." He can face it—he loves it. I attended a play Clayton staged, a one-man production of *Hamlet*. Clayton played all the characters, and although *Hamlet* is a sad and powerful piece of art, Clayton had infused humour—the unpredictable. He used balloons for all the characters and as they died (by killing each other off!),

Balmoral Street

he popped the balloons—the message was both dramatically powerful and tragic, yet the drama also had a hint of humour as balloon after balloon popped in the frantic climactic rampage. Clayton combined comedy and tragedy—the opposite sides of the same coin, simply by using balloons. It's how we all live.

Clayton is devoted to creating theatre that is not elite; his vision of theatre is for the general public's experience. Superior art is actually not elitist, so Clayton and his theatre company focus on providing non-cliquey theatre; you begin by entering the "lobby," a little room with local art hung on the white walls, often done by a group of challenged adults. When I saw his *Hamlet*, the walls were hung with art painted by people with brain injuries. You buy your ticket from a quiet man at a plywood table, and then for a small donation, you can have coffee and locally baked morsels (which Clayton even serves).

Then you go into the dark theatre draped with black cloth around the small stage. There are bathrooms at the back and Clayton said there have been some minor renovations backstage so that actors won't have to run across the street to the inn to change into their costumes. The seats are basic chairs, not red velvet.

The plays are extremely professional, and could sometimes perhaps be disturbing, but what do we call disturbing? Do they make you think about life? That may not be as disturbing as we think—it may be productive. Why is it that we can watch a disturbing film, but find the closeness of humanity in a theatre so much more difficult?

You never know what to expect or what you may feel or experience at Theatre Inconnu. It's just as Emily at The Paint Box and I said, you never know what's around the corner and when you might catch it—a delightful surprise may await you at one of Clayton's plays, a new thought that might change our world!

Fernwood truly is a cultural and artistic hub, but it's more than that; it's a place that understands our vulnerabilities, our highs and lows, the momentary leaping of our hearts, our great woes. People in Fernwood seem to know that we are as fragile as a bubble or a balloon, with thin nerves so easily broken, or a tender seedling, but also as tenacious as an earthworm on its way to a warm bundle of microbes, a ukulele band playing a maritime jig, or a strong Turkish coffee. Fernwood feels the human spirit and it attracts people whose emotions are close to the surface—they wear their hearts on their sleeves, and maybe that's why art and nature play such a major role in this neighbourhood. People here are not afraid of feeling what it means to be human, and art and nature are their strength.

Royal Jubilee Hospital: Surprise Treasures!

The Royal Jubilee Hospital is only a few blocks east of Fernwood Village and has recently undergone some very attractive renovations—it reminded me of the Vancouver airport with great sunlit lobbies, waterfalls, public art, and curved wooden reception counters.

Down a few hallways and up the elevator you come upon a beautiful, sun-drenched courtyard atop a rocky knoll nestled amongst the new brick-and-glass towers. Here you may visit the historic Pemberton Memorial Chapel, dating back to 1909 and lovingly restored in 1998 by the Royal Jubilee Hospital School of Nursing Alumnae.

The chapel is a dear little brick structure and well worth a quiet visit. It is surrounded by a fragrant Victorian-styled garden, patios, and benches, as well as a Japanese garden. Amongst the lavender beds and simple elegant stones is also the restored Pemberton Memorial Operating Room, a National Heritage Site. Joseph Despard Pemberton was the first surveyor general of Vancouver Island.

Who would have ever thought that you could visit a hospital for entertainment purposes? And how civil it is, how compassionate and sophisticated, to include these beautiful gardens and historic features within our hospital facility.

ROXY

ANONYMOUS 915 A VERY HAROLD & KUMAR XMAS

Quadra Street near Hillside Avenue

CHAPTER SIX

Quadra

It's a funny thing, but quite often the largest and most normal working family neighbourhoods are ignored for exactly this reason, that they are quiet and modest and people go about their day-to-day business and there seems to be nothing original or spectacular or culturally unique in these areas. This applies, for instance, to the Quadra area north of downtown, spreading northward into the peninsula toward the highway and the Saanich suburbs.

Perhaps it is exactly the quiet, normal lifestyle of these hard-working families that is in fact unique; we wouldn't have a city without these neighbourhoods like Quadra, which are made up of quiet, tree-lined streets, modest family homes with bikes and toys on the front lawn, men washing the car on the weekends, and unpruned lilacs falling onto the sidewalks where children have done chalk drawings and played hopscotch. There are numerous recreational athletic parks and basketball courts where soccer and ball games are played by the local youth after school as they trudge home from public schools with loaded backpacks.

Natural, scenic landscaped parks and gardens in this neighbourhood are not as common as in the seashore neighbourhoods. The parks in the Quadra area serve a purpose other than for strolling and looking at nature—they serve families. There are community centres that hold "teen barbecue nights" and day camps in the summer. Sinewy boys glide along the sidewalks and jump off the curbs on their beaten-up skateboards. Mothers keep watch over their toddlers playing in the sandboxes in the numerous pocket playgrounds, and young girls in sparkly pink T-shirts talk together on the sidewalks as they amble home from school.

This large neighbourhood is not fancy, nor does it have a "poor but proud" feeling, but rather, it just *is*. The Quadra lifestyle is simply just how we all live day to day, taking care of our families, friends, homes, lawns, and cars, playing sports, paying our taxes, holding garage sales or barbecues for the neighbourhood baseball team, going out to dinner nearby on the weekend, returning books to the library, taking swimming lessons at the local pool, shovelling snow on the rare day in winter when we get it, building a snowman in the front yard. There is something secure about normalness, something calm and nice about creating and living a life based on the routine of having a job and a family and a home.

Quadra Street is long, running from downtown all the way out to the highway, the length of Victoria, actually. At the downtown end, there are numerous heritage churches—huge old brick-and-stone structures with steeples, grand carved entrances, and stained-glass windows. A block farther north there are just as many *new* churches.

Up Quadra past the churches there are practical shops and services; this is what the Quadra neighbourhood is: practical, down-to-earth, and family oriented. There is a bicycle shop, a tax service, a medi-chair and scooter outlet, and a funeral-planning place where you can select your coffin!

A little farther along is Victoria's new police station. It's a beautiful, streamlined reddish-brown building and the most striking feature about the exterior is the public art on the corner; it's a sculpture of five people (two are women) holding up a giant, rectangular slab of smooth, white polished rock; the people are leaning with all their might to keep the slab from crushing them. It's called *Trust and Harmony*. Inside the station is a small museum jammed with police memorabilia, including old handcuffs, smelling salts, and a rubber contraption resembling a primitive form of some sort of squirt bottle. There's an old 1938 Harley-Davidson motorbike with a sidecar, and Victoria's first automated traffic light, large and cumbersome and painted dark green—it stood on the corner of Douglas and Johnson Streets in 1935.

Just beyond the police station is the aged Victoria Curling Rink, which is still used and not just for curling; its enormous, hollow, dim space is home to the giant *Times Colonist* book sale, a fantastic annual event that raises money for literacy. The first year I went, I stood in a long line and watched people wheeling out stacks of books on dollies and in carry-on luggage, and I thought, "Wow, those people are obsessed with books; I'll only buy one or two," but when I got to the massive, musty-smelling rink with its fluorescent lighting and scuffed walls, I couldn't pull myself away and finally left with two boxes of beautiful, hardcover books that each cost one dollar! One of the books I found was an old nature book from 1932 with lovely coloured illustrations of strange animals and their habits. The fries and burgers at the rink canteen are very good too.

The Quadra neighbourhood has a "village" which makes an interesting stroll in daylight hours (that's when everything is open). It even has new and handsome purple street banners. The village is a few blocks long and is a colourful mix of ethnic restaurants, secondhand shops, a bridal dress shop and a hydroponics store. There's the Sparkle Bright Laundromat with immense amounts of steam coming from the pipes on the roof and blowing over the used-book store, and the old retro Roxy Theatre, which still regularly shows feature films.

The art-school students up the street are planting a medicinal herb garden called "The People's Apothecary" in the large lot behind their graffiti-painted school. They proudly held an open house on a cold, raw May afternoon and showed us the plans for the newly dug and mulched plot. The ambitious students have planted dill for indigestion, sumac for impotence and asthma, and raspberries to help "prepare the uterus for childbirth" (presumably one would eat them?).

On the village bulletin board is an invitation to immigrants to drop into the Immigrant Centre nearby. The Quadra neighbourhood is home to many new Canadians—it's a multicultural neighbourhood. In the village you can eat Asian kabobs, Chinese duck, Greek souvlaki, Caribbean stew, or Italian pizza. Farther along there is an Italian bakery and a Manila video store, an "Asian Emporium," and a Mediterranean store full of cheeses, Turkish delight, nuts, spices, pastas, grape leaves, dried fruit, and shelves of colourful cans of olive oil and tomatoes.

There's a romance to an ethnic neighbourhood, a global, worldly, warm feeling amongst all the little food outlets with the smells of cooking wafting down the back alleys. In an ethnic neighbourhood, people are busy, food is being cooked, and there's a good kind of human energy—hard, raw, working energy. This is what it means to be human, to be alive, all together with our different global traditions.

One unique heritage feature of the Quadra neighbourhood is its history of the garage! Originally, carriages were kept in carriage houses, but when the car came into fashion garages began to be built; eventually, the garage became attached to the house. "Cars began to move into the house," says a local brochure on the history of the Quadra neighbourhood. And this in turn led to urban sprawl and suburban development because this design altered the footprint of the home—more room was needed for building when the garage was attached to the house.

The detached garages, carriage houses, or garden sheds are often more charming than the main houses; one might have an old crooked weathervane on its peak, another an ancient climbing rose leaning on its southern side, crawling under the gables, or a little window with original glass and windowsill standing the test of time.

Farther north up Quadra, near the McKenzie intersection, are more shops. Amongst these modern and attractive stores is a genuine old farm store, Borden Mercantile, which still sells items in burlap sacks, and corn, pea, and bean seeds in bulk, displayed in colourful pails. You can buy an antiseptic lanoline cream for a cow's chapped udder, tractor parts, fish fertilizer, brass hooks and snaps, and bird feeders. In the earthy-smelling store there are faded posters on the wall of poultry breeds and the anatomy of the pig, and racks of flower seeds and stacks of livestock feed, including bags labelled Wet Nurse, a milk substitute for newborn livestock who have been rejected by their mothers.

At the northernmost part of Quadra Street is Rithet's Bog, which buffers the neighbourhood of Broadmead, a newer suburb that stretches over the rocky bluffs and then slopes down toward Cordova

Bay. The bog was donated by the Guinness family in 1994 as a nature sanctuary, and a group of devoted citizens has taken on the stewardship of the bog (with the Saanich Parks Department). Their most recent restoration project was to cut back a very aggressive, invasive bulrush, which if left unchecked would quickly grow over the entire wetland.

Rithet's Bog is a peat bog. Peat bogs all over the world are diminishing; they are either being drained and developed or, more likely in many countries, the peat is being removed to be used as fuel or for horticultural purposes. Peat bogs form over thousands of years from decaying plants in a wet and poorly drained watershed. As plants decay, and the water and soil develop a high acidity level, plants such as sphagnum moss and other vegetation, insects, grasses, and fungi thrive and also die and decay, creating the bog and the layers of peat. Peat can actually be the first stage of coal development. Some bogs, such as Rithet's, are called "domed bogs" because the centre is raised from the heavy buildup of material—in Rithet's, the dome consists of coniferous vegetation.

It takes about an hour to stroll around the lovely gravel trail at Rithet's Bog; on one side is a mass of bulrushes and willows, reeds and grasses, and then the trail takes you through the damper, darker, more forested section where dead trees are rotting back into the earth amongst the ferns and pines and dense native shrubs such as Indian plum and snowberries.

Throughout the walk there is a distinctive smell—a fresh, soft odour of natural decay, of nature working with all her microbes to decompose everything in the bog; the smell reminded me vaguely of Gran's kitchen in summer at dinnertime, when we'd have boiled peas from her garden and new potatoes with mint. Decay does not have to be foul-smelling—in a bog it is a wonderful, working whiff that filters through the thick growth that Mother Nature is labouring on.

Rithet's Bog is named after the prominent Scottish businessman (and mayor of Victoria from 1884 to 1885) Robert Rithet, who owned much of the land in the area and bred racehorses in the early 1900s. One of his most famous horses was in fact named Broadmead, which really does sound like a winner. Rithet's businesses were shipping, flour, steel, real estate, canning, and Hawaiian sugar.

Rithet drained the bog (which originally was a source of cranberries) for agricultural purposes, using his draft horses, which had to wear large flat wooden shoes so they didn't sink in the mud. As soon as agricultural production ceased, however, Mother Nature quickly took the cultivated field back to the deep, wet, decaying bog that it truly wanted to be, for all of us to enjoy.

West Bay Marina

CHAPTER SEVEN

Up the Gorge, Vic West, and View Royal

The Gorge is a waterway running about four miles up from the Inner Harbour to a wide bay called Portage Inlet. The Gorge has immense diversity and history and can be visited by kayak or canoe, bicycle, on the chubby little harbour ferries, on foot, or by car.

First, let it be said that in the Victoria region, one is never at a loss for things to do, to attend, and to learn. In Victoria's "heritage week," I saw a small announcement inviting the public to attend a lecture and slide show at the public library in the Gorge area on the history of the Gorge. If you make the effort to dress for the cold weather and drive through the dark, wet streets on a drizzly, raw February evening to learn about our city, you will not be disappointed.

I bundled up and crossed town to hear a gentle and educated man speak on the topic. I parked and braced myself against the cruel wind as I made my way across the dark parking lot and into the warm and friendly library—the little talk and slide show were to be in a cozy corner, and there were coffee and soft chairs. The speech was only an hour long and the old photographs were amusing and interesting—I was so glad that I had made the effort to go to this modest event with perhaps a dozen other people. It was a comfort, an escape from the bitter winter and day-to-day stresses. There is something very secure and good about a library: one just assumes that everyone who goes to libraries is intelligent and thoughtful—there is nothing bad about a library!

At the lecture I learned about the terrible disaster on the Point Ellice Bridge (the Bay Street Bridge) on May 26, 1896. The bridge collapsed as a streetcar made its way across, loaded down with one hundred and forty-three vacationers heading up the Gorge to celebrate Queen Victoria's

birthday. Fifty-five people were unable to escape and died.

Grand and wealthy homes once lined the waterway, owned by beer barons, coal industrialists, judges, and socialites. Swimming parties, teas, picnics, and regattas were held regularly. There were brass bands on barges, dugout-canoe races of the First Nations, boat races between the British and Canadian navies, and cruises up the Gorge for ten cents, which included tea and piano playing (the piano was towed!). Tourists and visitors arrived by streetcar, or paddlewheeler, or horse and buggy, and some walked along the forest trails and often camped for the night. There were outdoor movies, a bandshell, swimming races, lemonade stands, and a bathing house for recreational swimming. To create a beach feeling, a barge full of sand was towed up the Gorge. (Times haven't really changed—the popular tourist beach in Waikiki in Honolulu, Hawaii, and the luxurious white beaches along Mexico's east coast south of Cancun are both enhanced by man-made sandy beaches.)

There was an amusement park with high-diving displays, which some thought was a bit dangerous given the shallow waters of the Gorge, and indeed, a diving accident did occur. Swimming clubs held backstroke races and the competitors had to hold a candle in their teeth! Three-mile swimming marathons were held from the Inner Harbour up the

Gorge and swimmers swam through the pollution of the time, which was described as swimming through "cigars."

Nowadays, we are all afraid of E. coli and related germs, but we weren't back then. I remember spending summers with Gran on Galiano Island and swimming all day in a lovely warm cove just below her cottage. The colourful, thriving sea life enchanted me and gave me my lifelong love of ocean ecology and biology. Years later, I realized why the cove was so warm and home to so many diverse species of sea life—it was where Gran's septic pipe emptied into the sea. There were far fewer chemicals in the septic systems then.

I don't know what type of pollution is in the Gorge today—perhaps it is cleaner than when the "cigars" were buoyant, or perhaps it contains more toxins, but we need to ask at some point, "What do we actually mean by clean?"

Many artifacts have been found in the Gorge from the days of long ago, sunk deep in the mud at low tide; old bottles, pottery, swimming tokens and the like have been retrieved through the sport of "mudlarking." Today, mudlarking is replaced by those who stroll the beaches with metal detectors.

There is a dedicated group of people who call themselves The Gorge Waterway Initiative; their mission is to protect and restore health to the Gorge waterway. They give the Gorge a big clean-up every year, as well as monitoring stormwater drainage, and work to preserve bird and wildlife habitat. Their informative booklet notes that the little native oysters and the local herring population both need the Gorge to survive and thrive. The group also restores the shoreline.

A very interesting bicycle ride or walk up the Gorge begins at the west end of the Johnson Street Bridge. The flat, paved route takes you up the beginning of the Gorge along a newly developed part of town called Selkirk Water. What was an industrial area of old red-brick warehouses and factories is now a modern and pristine array of great glass-and-concrete condominiums with balconies and paving-stone courtyards and beautifully landscaped potted trees. It is difficult for me to decide which is lovelier, the crumbling warehouses with their yellowed windows and tangled mass of urban wild growth crawling over the old stone walls, or the modern, energy-efficient towers with their planned and immaculate green roofs and plug-in depots for electric cars.

Across the waterway and farther along toward the Bay Street Bridge, the city is still very much industrial. Heaps of recycled cars, barges loaded with gravel secured with thick ropes bobbing against huge, stolid wharves, and sparks streaking like fireworks from welders repairing huge brass propellers form the view behind the numerous pilings and docks across the dark water. I find this busy, rugged, working place intriguing, and strangely austere and lovely. I would rather look at a heap of recycled, crushed cars and men in overalls working on cranes than a car lot full of new and shiny vehicles and red balloons and men in little suits, with cell phones, smelling of sweet aftershave.

Years ago, when Mum was visiting me, a nice man offered to paddle us down the Gorge in his canoe to the Inner Harbour to the annual Symphony Splash ("Victoria really knows how to have fun!" Mum said). We drifted quietly down the Gorge at dusk in his canoe, wrapped in blankets and drinking his homemade pear wine (he'd given us a gallon jug of it with two plastic glasses). The evening sky was a deep blue and the water was black and still as we made our way past the gulls silhouetted atop the pilings and the bobbing fishboats with a faint glow from the portholes at water level. That's my memory of the Gorge. The symphony was wonderful and the green and pink fireworks that lit up the sky were exciting, but they masked the night sky—the stars and the skyline. The memorable event was slipping quietly down the dark, resting, lapping Gorge, sipping that pear wine and looking up at the great, silent mountains of industrial work under that vast blue night sky.

The industrial area soon merges into a pretty area of new and tasteful townhomes and cafés joined by walkways and small pocket parks. On the western side, clusters of colourful modular homes dot the waterfront, and interpretive nature and heritage signage provides you with a good education on local nature and history. There are small landscaped rest stops, benches, drinking fountains, and information kiosks with route maps. The signage points out ecological restoration projects and native species that you might see—it's fun to take along binoculars on these excursions.

The Selkirk Trestle used to be a railway bridge. On one side of the trestle is a piece of the original wooden pipe that was part of the historic water system in Victoria when water was piped into town. Cafés, canoe clubs, small parks, and urban pathways line both sides of the Gorge.

Vic West

The quirky, historic neighbourhood of Vic West is easy to miss because it's on top of the slope. Its rolling, grassy meadow of Banfield Park borders the Gorge, but if you make your way up through the park under the Garry oak trees, a delightful village and heritage neighbourhood await your visit.

In the park is a storage container painted by the local residents with broad brush strokes reading WELCOME TO VICTORIA WEST. There's a modest community centre in the park with a children's summer camp schedule posted on its outside

bulletin board; children may attend pirate camps where they can "walk the plank," or bug camps where they can play spider soccer, or space camps where they build their own alien egg—somebody at the community centre is very creative.

Across the street is a row of shops—a hemp store and a children's consignment shop, often with pretty little sundresses hanging in the window. The hair salon doubles as an art gallery displaying beautiful pottery for sale in the window, and the barber's sign in the door lists "free hot lather neck shaves" and military haircuts.

But the main centre of activity is at the Spiral Café with its oiled, planked floor and wooden tables, delicious lattes, and yellow wall covered with children's art. The day I was there, the art, some of it looking like what Picasso was striving for, was strong and bold with titles such as *Pink Lady* and *Lifting Up Bird*. There was a rather abstract painting of the Golden Gate Bridge—abstract without the artist (a child) knowing it was abstract, with big bold orange swaths of colour—you just knew it was the massive bridge but it was simply rich shapes. On a cool Saturday afternoon, the café was cozy and warm; a tarnished glitter ball hung off a leafy plant beside an old battered white piano, which was played by a man with a grey ponytail singing about a long-lost love.

Everywhere you look in the Vic West neighbourhood, there are lush gardens. Outside the community centre are Oregon grape bushes with boughs bending, full of plump, purple fruit—they are the largest Oregon grapes I have ever seen. The community centre's public garden is full of herbs, strawberries, bee balm, and goji. Goji is considered a "superfood"—it's in every health magazine I pick up. It's a little red berry from Asia and is said to strengthen the legs and aid in fertility, among other things.

On the corner beside the community centre is another garden, a public garden full of fruit trees, flowers, fennel, and artichokes as big as my fist. You can walk amongst the growth on a little path, but be careful of the numerous and busy bees enjoying this jungle of flowers and food!

Just around the corner from the café, up on Fullerton Avenue, is the huge Salvation Army High Point Community Church. They have a community garden as well where the peas spill out onto the sidewalk; the church not only grows food in their raised beds but also harvests it and gives it to those in need. There are more community gardens behind the café too, where cucumber and trailing squash vines have escaped from the plots and trail along the sidewalk.

Another shop not to be missed is the antique store just up the road from the hub of shops and the Spiral Café. It is chock-a-block full of what I would call attic treasures—silver hairbrushes, cut-glass perfume bottles, red-velvet footstools, and bedroom sets that look as if they came right out of Jane Austen's house. But their specialty is lamps and lampshades; from floor to ceiling are silk shades with fringes, great turbans, brass pole lamps, hand-painted porcelain oil lamps, crystal sconces, glittering chandeliers, and milk-glass reflectors. It is truly magical.

Of course the heritage homes with their old porches, solid wood doors, climbing roses, and stained-glass windows are a lovely sight. One of the girls who drive the horse carriages in James Bay told me that the stained-glass windows were shipped from England and packed in barrels of molasses for protection, but the lead from the windows soaked into the molasses and the residents got lead poisoning.

Vic West is a delightful addition to the Gorge excursion, an array of historic and eclectic businesses on quiet streets where everyone is welcome and where gardens thrive.

View Royal

The Gorge continues, eventually ending on Portage Inlet where the municipality of View Royal begins. This was one of the first settled areas of Victoria, rich in history with one of the most charming and scenic shorelines—many original fruit trees and little groves of wildflowers line the narrow lanes, and there are two original community halls, which volunteers lovingly care for.

View Royal sits on the Old Island Highway, an original stagecoach route that travelled from town out toward Sooke. There are three historic pubs (the Four Mile, the Six Mile and the Seventeen Mile) on this route; some say they are the oldest pubs in the region (although I have also heard that the pub on Mayne Island, the Springwater, is the oldest).

The quaint and traditional British Four Mile Pub is in View Royal—as they get farther away from town, the pubs become, well, a bit less refined (some people like their pubs that way!). The village pub in View Royal is surrounded by pretty gardens and hanging baskets, and inside it is full of old lanterns, stained-glass windows, heavy oak furniture, and a sturdy, solid bar. Earthenware crocks and antiques sit on stone mantels, and many of the patrons on Sunday afternoon look as if they might be there for a pint after a tramp with their walking sticks across windswept moors. It's charming, and my friend even said that her Guinness tasted as good here as in Dublin. The pub's brochure proudly states that its catering business in "Creative Ice Sculptures, Ice Punch Bowls and Extensive Decorations puts them a cut above the rest!"

A highlight of View Royal is the stone wall across the road from the pub, built by a traditional Italian stonemason as part of the infrastructure improvement project when the road had to be

Cole Island, Esquimalt

widened. This is the most beautiful mosaic wall I have ever seen! It's a true piece of public art, made from a concrete base with slabs of vertical, pastel rectangular rocks and beach stones placed in wonderful swirling patterns that resemble beaches, sandbars, shells, tidal pools, and waves. "He would come to work in a little suit and tie with his lunch bucket, and chip away all day with his many chisels and hammers in the scorching heat as the traffic roared by, placing stones in intricate strategic places and tapping them into place," a man in the pub told me over his pint of golden ale under an old print of a hunting scene.

There's a funny juxtaposition or irony to View Royal as well; along the main highway there is a replica of a wooden fort with great yellow letters advertising it as Fort Victoria, but behind the grand fort is a large, sprawling trailer park. There is nothing wrong with that, but I just cannot quite make the connection between the trailers and the fort!

View in the name View Royal comes from the spectacular waterfront vistas of Esquimalt Harbour. In the harbour is a small island the View Royal residents love to protect by watching it with binoculars and paddling over in their kayaks to make sure it has not been abused or vandalized. Cole Island is part of the Esquimalt Naval Sites National Historic Site and houses Esquimalt's oldest buildings—wooden and brick structures built in 1858 to store gunpowder and shells; there is a little guard house as well. Age, sun, and sea salt have turned the red-brick walls a weather-washed pink, darker at the bottom where the calm water rises and ebbs, waiting for the naval boats to tie up and load their ammunition through the high arched entrances.

Perhaps the aesthetic appeal of heritage structures is enhanced with age—they are at their most beautiful just before they give in, like a jar of fading tulips on a sunny windowsill—there's a quiet peace about them, subtle and lovely, still enjoying the life around them, still hanging on but ready to go.

Funding by the federal government has been announced to preserve the old buildings on Cole Island, which is a delightful and welcome project.

At the Entrance to Esquimalt Harbour

CHAPTER EIGHT

Esquimalt

As you make your way up the Gorge and beyond Vic West, you will come to the municipality of Esquimalt. Esquimalt in the First Nations language means "place of shoaling waters." This area was once a traditional First Nations village and a rich source of shellfish, most likely because of the shoaling, or shallow, water.

If ever a place had a mistaken image or identity, it is Esquimalt. Of all our neighbourhoods in and around Victoria, Esquimalt is the most surprising because of what one assumes. Esquimalt is home to the Canadian Forces dockyards and naval base. Great yellow cranes in the shipyard can be seen across the water from James Bay and many other neighbourhoods. Part of it, Naden (the name of the base), is accessible to the public and you can take tours by foot or by a shuttle bus. Esquimalt village is simply a stretch of stores that includes two Tim Hortons, a bingo hall, a consignment shop,

a small strip mall, a pawn shop (I hear it is one of the best in town), and several pubs and other businesses. But behind the main street and naval base is a wonderful surprise!

There are quaint neighbourhoods of modest little homes with lovely front gardens on quiet streets that lead down to a beautiful park called Saxe Point. It runs along the sea, not overly manicured, but with wild semi-woodland trails full of salmonberry bushes, arbutus trees, and Oregon grape, interspersed with little sandy coves with rowboats tied by frayed yellow ropes to washed-up logs.

Toward Victoria is Macaulay Point, a huge, breezy bluff, dramatic and windswept, with a meadow-like landscape that looks out over the grey-green sea dotted with boats, ferries, and cruise ships. Lovely, neat, cedar split-rail fences guide you along gravel pathways and also protect areas of native plants that the town is trying to encourage.

At the municipal hall you can pick up a thick but neat package of maps and brochures of different strolls and walks through Esquimalt. The pamphlets are wonderfully illustrated with historic photographs, and the map routes are easy to follow. There's a walk through the Gorge area, the West Bay community (where the houseboats tie up and the mayor has her floating physiotherapy clinic), and other lovely walks that include parks, public art (be sure to see the First Nations mural on the side of the municipal hall), gardens, memorials, footpaths, beaches, heritage and First Nations features, art deco and Tudor revival architecture, and quiet lanes.

One of the most interesting walks is through Old Esquimalt, which begins at the Lampson Street School. The school was originally a four-room brick building built in 1903. The walk through this historic area takes you up through Cairn Park to the highest point in Esquimalt at

232.25 feet. The trail ambles through the Garry oak meadows between great black rock faces and patches of bluebells and fawn lilies. At the top is a stone cairn with a tarnished, circular plaque that points out numerous viewpoints and sites around the region, including First Nations reserves, the shipyards, old railway routes, and elements of the local topography.

The landscapes in and around Victoria offer such a variety of perspectives. Your perspective changes dramatically depending on where you are looking from. Paddling a kayak along the seashore or up the Gorge, riding a bicycle path through a rose garden, and hiking up a rock face offer quite different views—you notice (or miss) different features of the cultural and natural landscape and the people in it, depending on your mode of transportation. But that's the beauty of Victoria—it begs you to explore all of its neighbourhoods by all means of movement.

On the walk down from Cairn Park you can travel along the "oldest planned road in the west," Old Esquimalt Road, constructed by sailors in 1852. On this particular walk, the feeling I absorbed seemed much more important than what there was to learn. Sometimes, what you see and learn on a walking tour is not as important as that mysterious ambience you experience just by being surrounded by an area's features. You can study the information before or after, but if you just walk and observe and enjoy the area, you might find that that is enough. Of all the walking that I do, this area is one of the most memorable, not because of the facts, but because of its feeling.

Esquimalt is a place where facts are not as important as feeling and ambience. There's something about the place that fascinates—those windswept, grassy bluffs and the funny old streets, the railway yards, the little wartime homes, the military hospital up on the hill, the spectacular scenery mixed with the giant yellow cranes in the shipyards, the houseboats and floating homes just down the lane from the Naval Officer Training Centre. It's a place of contrasts, of rough mixed with smooth, wild with manicured, and tradition with modern, and all with a hint of mystery and the unknown. These are feelings you cannot absorb by reading a pamphlet of historical facts; you just have to wander this neighbourhood and enjoy the diversity.

I have always found military and naval lifestyles (as well as the Sisters and their convent lives) very mysterious and secretive. It seems to be a strangely protected life where one feels taken care of; that's a nice secure feeling, but at the same time it's rather odd to be protected by such structure and routine.

You might never think it, but the navy and the Sisters have a lot in common. They both practise an intense discipline, usually behind closed doors; they both wear rather curious outfits (most nuns don't actually still wear habits); they both rely enormously on teamwork; they both hold a great deal of faith; they are both gender based; and they both, I would expect, are a challenge to enter and a challenge to leave—opposite sides of the same coin! But it's that mysterious life they both lead that is so intriguing. They seem more secretive than a spy or a private investigator because they are more visible within society than spies but you still don't truly know what they do in their worlds.

Part of the naval base is accessible to the public but much is private. You go through the great

Saxe Point

Esquimalt Municipal Hall

red-brick gates at Naden and up on your left is the store—they have their own *store*! You can buy everything from a waterproof notepad to big boxer shorts to raspberry candies. They have their own gym and skating rink, and there's even a little sailing school down the hill at the back of an old building in a gritty parking lot. Naden has a wonderful band too. I never stopped to think about how valuable a band is to the military, but it is, not only for ceremonial purposes, but for the mood of the military, especially during conflict—it's moving to think of the band playing in the midst of a horrific war. The band is also a link between the outside world and the gated world of the military; the musicians act as ambassadors to their military bases, connecting in a small way from our lives to theirs.

The dockyard is off-limits to us, but you can drive or stroll throughout the Naden base, which is a twisting array of little roads, red-brick heritage buildings, and pockets of grassy knolls and shrubbery including a huge, blazing-red rhododendron in front of the library. It's a strange little community. I cannot pinpoint exactly why I find it so intriguing, but it is; there's an air of mystery about the place, a mystery combined with an order amongst all this history, with a dark submarine just down the hill, snug against the dock in the off-limits area (probably being repaired) and our grey frigates anchored out in the harbour mist.

The military museum on the base is excellent. It is housed in an old brick building with white trim, yellowed windows, and white columns along a veranda or porch—it looks like something from the Deep South. Heavy bronze radiators heat the musty, carpeted hallway and dim rooms, which are light blue with white wainscoting. There are all sorts of naval memorabilia and displays. In the dark, cave-like Communications Room is a worn poster with red lettering of OFFICIAL SECRETS; there is a photograph of Mollie Entwistle receiving a medal for her "conspicuous coolness and courage" in rescuing people from a fire in the mess hall; there are displays of intricate knots including the "Granny Bend" and the "Single Marriage Bend"; there is a muster kit and the list, in alphabetical order, of supplies a soldier could sign out. Under *H* is "house wife!" I asked a passing sergeant if this was a joke and he chuckled and said, "Well, let's put it like this. If the army wanted you to have a wife, they would have issued you one."

There is a ditty box, a small wooden box for the soldiers to keep their personal treasures in (everyone should have a ditty box, a little secret piece of privacy); an old rusted ration kit that includes a little package of biscuits and a Bible; and, in a battered wooden frame hanging on the wall, a photograph of our first Canadian First Nations woman to sign up, Private Mary Grey Eyes from Saskatchewan.

In another room was a travelling exhibit on naval mascots—animals! There were wonderful photographs of men in their white sailor suits scrubbing the decks with a little white goat keeping watch, or a big cat lying in its own hammock with one leg hanging over the edge. One boat even had a dexterous bear cub who liked to sit on the bow, and there were Gus the goose, dogs, and a parrot too. Cats were especially popular, though, because they kept the rat population in check—rats chewed many a rope in the bowels of the ships.

Before leaving this charming museum (many other rooms were crammed with toy soldiers, brass bells, photographs of admirals, artifacts, land-mine maps, and rum bottles with labels from Waterloo, Ontario),

I signed the guest book in the hallway and picked up a few free brochures on the navy's history. I also picked up a gold and red pin that honours our Canadian soldiers, who not only go to war but are peacekeepers as well. How I wish Canada was more of a peacekeeper! I feel so proud of Canada for our kindness and modesty in the world, but my pride would double if we were still known as peacekeepers—I really think that peacekeeping is one of the noblest actions a country can take on. The pin is on my jacket, next to the art-gallery pin of the Shinto shrine.

As I left I took one more glance at a 1940s poster that encouraged women to sign up; it promised a great life, with good food, recreation facilities, friendship, and a future. Mum signed up and was a war artist—she says it was one of the greatest times of her life.

E&N Railway Roundhouse

Cadboro Bay from Sinclair Road

CHAPTER NINE

Cadboro Bay

My first "encounter" with and reason for going to Cadboro Bay was to do a book reading in the charming little bookshop (sadly, now closed) in Cadboro Bay Village. I was enchanted by a subtle sense of community, of oldness and tradition, of the ultimate village-ness of this rural neighbourhood that sits down the hill from the University of Victoria's vast forest lands and tasteful, coffee-coloured, modern student residences.

The Cadboro Bay Book Company was nestled amongst a few other little stores separated by tiny red-brick alleyways, which I learned are called "mouse holes" by the locals. An acquaintance of mine calls them "snickets." The word *snicket* is an old north-country British expression for an alleyway that is not a dead end. These snickets were tastefully cluttered with clay flower pots and ceramic containers of trailing shrubs and herbs and hanging moss baskets of geraniums. The little shops had freshly painted doors with decorative brass knockers and were selling beautiful items such as French soaps, handmade paper, and beeswax candles.

Next door to the bookshop was a dark and mysterious, burgundy-draped Russian restaurant—one could almost feel Rasputin's presence across the dark wood of the bar and through the yellowed wallpaper, over which hung some stained mirrors in heavy gilded frames. And to add even more austerity to the dark Slavic ambience, there was a crisp white business card beside the pyramid stack of highball glasses that read SECRET INVESTIGATIONS—PRIVATE INVESTIGATOR with a last name of Jones and a number. I put the card in my pocket—I was intrigued! I decided to contact this detective and I'll let you know later in this chapter what they do. I have always been fascinated by what private investigators really do. I hope it's more than spying on sad, aging men having affairs.

The next time I ventured down to Cadboro Bay, the restaurant had a FOR LEASE sign in the window and the burgundy drapes were closed.

At the pharmacy I bought a little book about the neighbourhood by a local author, Ursula Jupp. Peppers grocery store next door has won national community grocery store awards (in its category) for years, and the locals will proudly tell you that their prize-winning store is the hub and heart of Cadboro Bay. They can purchase everything from local island cheese to real imported English toffee under delightful signs that hang over each aisle and offer food trivia such as "The word onion is Latin and means giant pearl."

Cadboro Bay is named after a British ship, the *Cadboro* (the kind of ship from the mid-1800s with tall layers of white billowing sails), which anchored in the quiet bay where the Songhees people had established their fishing village along the sandy shore. In a recent excavation on a sheltered part of the beach, a copper shield was found. This finding could well date back to the voyages of Captain Vancouver in the late 1700s or even before his visit—that is the fascinating thing about archaeology, to figure out time—it's very philosophical. In his journals, Captain Vancouver describes the First Nations' love of copper and other metal objects.

Cadboro Bay Village is unique in that it sits practically on the beach, which arcs around the smooth sandy cove where little sailboats bob in the gentle waves. In nice weather, residents and visitors sit on the large driftwood logs that have washed up on the beach in the winter storms or stroll the beach (it's a great swimming beach as well).

Between the beach and the village is a vast green park that spans the length of the bay—this is Gyro Park, which used to be a huge marshy bog. It is actually slightly lower than sea level but has been filled in with "hog fuel" (leftover wood chips and bark from the local sawmill). The thing about hog fuel is that it breaks down, so in rainy weather Mother Nature has a bit of a laugh and Gyro Park turns into a shallow lake, which is still lovely if you have high rubber boots. There was once a grand

Olive Olio's

hotel on the Cadboro Bay waterfront, and there's a photograph of it hanging in the village pub, next to a glittering lottery machine. Within the park are three huge colourful sculptures of creatures for all to climb on—a giant red octopus, a blue whale, and the famous Cadborosaurus, a sea monster who is reported to be lurking in the deep, mysterious local waters. "We need a new sighting," said my guide and new friend Norman, "to keep the myth alive." (The last sighting was in 1981.)

As in many communities that sit on the water, whether lakes or seas, there have been sightings (by very normal people) of strange and primitive snake-like looped monsters. In Cadboro Bay, the locals affectionately call their monster "Caddy." In past

descriptions from local fishermen, the so-called monster was about eighty feet long and surfaced with his big clammy head, which resembled that of "a sheep or horse, not a cow," and it was "moving in coils, not slithering like a snake." The monster never did anyone harm. In fact, one can assume that he was a rather shy, gentle, timid creature, and perhaps he wasn't a monster after all, but a lonely, drifting sea creature whose appearance frightened the human species. We call him a monster because of his appearance, but perhaps his personality was one of passivity and fear.

The neighbourhood of Cadboro Bay is tightly bonded and there are several reasons for this. The first, according to some residents and business owners who live beside the lovely beach, is that they share the vulnerability of being in the most likely earthquake and tsunami area. If a tsunami ever occurs in our region, they fear that the volatile surf would sweep the entire village and nearby homes out to sea in an instant. The community is well prepared and is one of the few neighbourhoods in the region that has an emergency plan established by the residents! In case of "the big one," the neighbourhood has stockpiled (bolted in metal boxes in various locations) rubber totes of water, bandages, and colour-coded visors for the volunteers who all have specific tasks and skills. There is a chart of the locations of backhoes, wells, and places for helicopters to land, and there is a list of residents with special skills—the whole plan is based around the philosophy of "neighbour helping neighbour."

Another bonding factor is that Cadboro Bay is a part of Victoria history and settlement—great-nieces and grandchildren of original families still live in Cadboro Bay; apple trees and laneways and ponds and creeks are fiercely protected by the residents because their great-great-great-uncle used to fish in the creek, or their grandmother sat under the cherry tree in the park on a hot summer day. It is this past-rooted loyalty and sense of history that gives the place stability, a flavour of rich heritage of pride, and a determination to preserve the place for the future.

Norman (whom I met through the Cadboro Bay Business Association's website) and I strolled through the neighbourhood, and although it was indeed residential, it had a feeling of old country charm. You just knew that it used to be a country community of farms and pioneer families. Every garden contained old fruit trees and heirloom shrubbery, which gently blended in with the adjoining lanes, footpaths, public meadows, and local mossy woods.

We ambled under arbutus trees and between snowberry hedges, through Garry oak stands and old orchards, over brooks on little wooden bridges, and down earthy trails lined with licorice ferns and damp, drooping cedars, and yet schools and

homes and even a hospital were all nearby. There was a certain type of fresh and wild space, a big sky, and the smell of wet trees and the sea, of the nurse logs slowly rotting back into the earth, and I could hear woodpeckers at work in the forest. The golden autumn leaves of the cottonwoods and trembling aspens and poplars towered above, shimmering in the wind after a stormy autumn morning.

Norman walked me down the footpaths within all this lovely nature and we came upon the back of historic Goward House. Goward House was built in 1908 by the Goward family, who settled here from England. The family home was originally called "Woodlands." The Gowards led a lovely English country life in Cadboro Bay, painting watercolours of the countryside, rowing in the bay, picnicking at the little nearby coves, and taking holidays and rides in their carriage. Goward House today is a seniors' activity centre where there are classes in everything from Death and Taxes to Chinese Brush Painting. You can also join the Purls of Wisdom Knitting Club or the Sun Room Bridge Group. Inside it is warm and cozy, with big sunny rooms and a fireplace, and a nice little place to have lunch.

The receptionist at the desk was very welcoming and told me that she'd lived in the area all her life and how it had changed—she used to ride her horse, Little Joe, into the woods and go mushrooming just down the street with her grandmother. But you know, I think you could still do that! Well, you might have to trailer your horse over from the nearby rural road in the Blenkinsop Valley a few miles away, but you could certainly still go mushrooming. And actually, I don't think a horse trotting down the streets of Cadboro Bay would seem that out of place.

I don't know what it is about mushrooms—they remind me of clowns, sort of deep and dark, with an ounce of lurking humour. What is a clown thinking? What is a mushroom doing in the deep earth amongst the rotting leaves and microbes? Is it the unknown that makes it so mysterious, and the element of darkness? They both seem to belong to a mysterious underworld—until they come into the light, and then we love them. A clown

becomes happy and funny, and the mushroom produces a delicious fruit (apparently quite high in protein). Neither creature should be so macabre and misunderstood, because when you stop and think about it, the clown and the mushroom both represent a great and valuable life force; the clown is our human condition (well, maybe that *is* scary), and the mushroom is a great fertile-soil maker that enriches our earth and forest floor.

Cadboro Bay consists of a few other unique properties. Norman and I passed Queenswood, a quiet, fourteen-acre landscaped property, now owned by the University of Victoria, which began as a home for the young Sisters of St. Ann who were studying health care and education. The building was then a retirement home for older Victoria nuns, and in recent years the Sisters used the property as a peaceful urban retreat and shared its tranquility with the public, offering courses in gentle spiritual pursuits such as meditation and prayer, healing and well-being.

The building at Queenswood was designed in the shape of a human body; the residences are the legs, the hospitality centre is the heart, and the head houses the chapel. Some buildings cleverly succeed in imitating human anatomy, and others, I suppose, do not. Maybe the body and heart are easier to navigate than the brain—designing a brain building might be pushing one's luck!

Across the road from Queenswood are the

Haro Woods, which recently became, in large part, a public park, thanks to the persuasion of many loyal local naturalists and residents. Norman and I traipsed along the lovely grassy trails as the sun shone between the great trees. A group of enthusiastic mountain-biking youth had created discreet trails and humps throughout the forest; my sense is that they just *have* to do it; it's an obsession—they can't help it. It was what I did in my youth in the woods with my old horse Missy—I created little jumps from logs and branches to achieve that two-second thrill of sailing over the obstacle in perfect form. It's what drives us all, I think—to get completely in tune with our rhythm and with nature's rhythm at exactly the same moment. We see it in sports more obviously, but it exists in art and ideas and in community spirit too, a connection perfectly right at that moment between being human and being in the world. What bliss it is.

Norman and I came upon "the great slab of the Haro Woods." The slab is an enormous granite stone about which a myth exists. The great mossy stone sits stoically amongst a stand of fir trees. It is glacial, probably tossed or rolled as the glacier melted and now embedded in the forest floor. Norman reckons that, like an iceberg, seventy percent of it is underground. The local myth is that if you place your hands on the stone in a specific place, heat from deep within the

Earth, through this gentle giant slab, will enter your body and change your life.

"For the better?" I asked Norman.

"Not sure," he said, as we continued on our stroll.

Our next stop on Norman's informative and lovely scenic tour was Mystic Vale—what a beautiful name. It conjures a magical wood full of fairies and nymphs and delicate flowers and butterflies, all dancing in a pale blue mist. Mystic Vale is in fact a huge forested ravine owned by the University of Victoria, full of walking trails along a little creek, and in autumn covered in thick maple leaves, with afternoon shafts of sunlight jutting between the bare trees onto the forest floor. These warm golden streaks remind me of the annunciation scenes painted through the ages; the annunciation, March 25 (my birthday), is when the angel Gabriel floated from heaven within a radiant glow to inform Mary that she was pregnant. Whether we are religious or not, I think we all appreciate the glory and beauty that the sun brings, especially through the forest.

You can look at a natural setting as a place to walk or an ecosystem, perhaps in need of restoration, or both. Even though these lovely woods are owned by the university, many caring and knowledgeable local residents care for Mystic Vale. They can't help it—"We love our trees," said one of my guides, Elizabeth.

Continued on page 129

Mushrooms can be found in the cool autumn after the summer heat fades and the cold, damp nights descend through the mists and onto the meadows and into the forests. Mushrooms love organic matter, either in the fields where perhaps livestock dung has been deposited, or in the woods, particularly under trees where there is a decay of leaves, branches, and even dead animals. Mushrooms in the forest are one of nature's most wonderful partnerships because the mushrooms help break down organic matter, thus enhancing the woodland soil for other plants.

There are many types of mushrooms with odd names such as the mouse pee pink gill and the stinkhorn, which emits a foul odour resembling rotting flesh. It attracts animals, which will eat it and then spread its spores through their feces—trust Mother Nature to come up with such an original way to spread herself around! It's one of her jobs.

Local Mushrooms

Mushroom gathering is perhaps one of the oldest forms of outdoor recreation and food harvesting, and it's a great surprise to find an edible wild mushroom hiding in the grass or under fallen pine needles. BUT, you need to know which mushrooms are edible, of course! Mushroom gatherers guard their special spots with a vengeance. A good mushroom is a true delicacy.

Here are three common, delicious wild mushrooms that grow in the Victoria region (ask a mushroom expert before you eat a wild mushroom, just to be sure!). The meadow mushroom is very common. It is white, with pink gills, and is found in open meadows and grasslands, lawns and boulevards. It is especially tender and delicious when it first pushes through the earth and is a little button shape. The shaggy mane also sprouts up from fertile grassy areas and is also white but tall and slender with a nice oval cap that looks shaggy, as if it has strings trailing from its top. The shaggy mane ages quickly and turns into a black liquid—some people call it the inky cap. I think the sexiest of all the wild mushrooms is the boletus, a thick, stout mushroom with a slimy, amber skin and a deep yellow spongy underside—you can't miss the spongy part. Boletus prefers to be under or near the woods, especially conifers. When cooked, the texture is much like tofu, sort of rubbery. BE CAREFUL—there are many types of this voluptuous mushroom and they are all good, except one.

Of course there are the little puffballs as well, which are fun to fry but rather tasteless. The white-spotted red toadstool, which we all have seen in children's books, is the fly agaric (agaric meaning mushroom) and is usually found in birch or pine forests. It is poisonous! Folklore has it that the red cap was placed in a saucer of milk and used to repel flies.

If mushrooming in our region appeals to you, consult an expert or obtain a mushroom book, and contact the South Vancouver Island Mycological Society for lots of information, courses, and events.

Truffles

Truffles are delicious, rare mushrooms that grow underground among the roots of willows, oaks, elms, chestnuts, and pines. Yes, they can be found on Vancouver Island, in the Douglas-fir forests, but the superior truffles are found in France and Italy. Female pigs were used historically to snuff out truffles. They were attracted to the musty smell of the underground morsel because it resembled the odour of a boar. Dogs are used now because the sows found the truffles to be a lovely snack.

I just cannot let this subject of the sexual sows go without a slight interjection. Having kept four dear, affectionate and loving, sweet-smelling sows at one time, as well as their beautiful and kind (albeit grizzled, hairy, slobbery, yellow-tusked) husband named Boris, I need to reflect for a moment on the odour of a boar, and therefore a truffle. I have never smelled a truffle, but Boris the boar had a ranky, musty odour combined with sort of a sweetness, perhaps from the alfalfa I fed him—his breath was clean, like fresh leaves. So, frankly, it's a compliment to our close relation, the pig, to favour a delicacy that smells like a boar. In a moment of reflection on why we value so highly a food that smells like a male pig's privates, I wondered what food could compare to a perspiring man's odour? And I think I have the answer—cashew butter!

Woodland Birds

As I grow older, I love birds more and more. I love their modesty, their work ethic, their creativity, their strength, and their wisdom. Cadboro Bay, being so forested and treed with its many parks, foreshore green spaces, and trails, is home to many birds. Here are three of my favourites.

Wrens: The wren is both hard-working and creative. There are several species but the one that you might see in the woods is the Pacific wren. This is a very inventive bird because it seeks out interesting places to nest and to make a home. You might find that your woodpile or rusted, abandoned rototiller has been converted into a nesting spot; the nest looks like a cup of sticks lined with leaves or soft feathers. A distinguishing feature of the wren is that it holds its tail upright.

The Pacific wren has a cousin, the winter wren, that lives near our many watercourses. The male winter wren will weave and build numerous nests from reeds and grasses to impress his wife. Should he be lucky enough to be accepted by her, the wedding will take place and she will select which abode she prefers. Each nest is constructed in a ball shape with a little hole for entering and exiting, well hidden in marsh or lakeshore grasses. Now how many husbands will do that for a potential mate and risk being rejected?

Great Horned Owl: The private, quiet, and patient one.

The great horned owl is distinguished by his handsome, large ear tufts. He sits in the trees and is active mostly in the evening. Sometimes in the night you can hear his "Whoo-hoo-oo," which for me seems very comforting, knowing that there is a presence deep in the trees when the rest of world is asleep. The great horned owl is a recycler, nesting in older, used nests in the trees constructed by other birds such as crows.

Owls perch very quietly on a limb, perhaps dozing or perhaps waiting to pounce on a morsel, but it is this focused stillness that has given them the image of wisdom; to be rash and impulsive may not be unwise, but to exhibit the owls' stoic dignity is admirable—I'd love to have their patience!

Swallows: Swallows are wonderfully busy little birds that eat *a lot* of insects by snatching them in their rapid, swooping, erratic flight. Swallows are very useful because many of the insects they consume, such as mosquitoes, are annoying to us.

The largest local swallow in North America is the purple martin. There is a dedicated birding group that is concerned about the purple martins' decline and has embarked on a large-scale plan to set up nesting boxes in many locations to help increase their population and bring

Continued from page 125

them home. Many of these locations are near the water, where insects are abundant.

On the Saanich Peninsula you can find the barn swallow with his chestnut throat and belly. The barn swallow builds nests of mud (and good peninsula clay!) on rafters inside barns and farm buildings. They pick up hair, wool, and feathers from the livestock below. But it is the violet-green swallow you will see in the woodlands and parks. In sunlight, the green shimmers like emeralds; the violet colour is on his backside. They make nests in tree cavities but will welcome a home inside a nesting box as well.

A word about nesting boxes—a friend of mine cleaned out her box when the babies had fledged and found the nest had a lining skilfully constructed of cigarette butts! I'm not sure what to think about this—it's an image I cannot get out of my head. It's sad in a way, and yet practical—it probably made a very warm nest. I'm not sure what would be more important to a bird preparing a nest for her young: warmth from toxic cigarette butts or a colder nest made from natural leaves and twigs.

Some of the activities of restoring a woodland ecosystem include planting natural native buffer areas around the woodland, removing invasive species (plant and animal), restricting access to sensitive areas, protecting nesting sites, controlling surface and groundwater flow from nearby homes, and maintaining natural drainage patterns. Believe it or not, a managed fire can be useful, to remove invasive plants and rejuvenate the soil (and it gives the local fire department a bit of extra practice).

On our way back to the village from Mystic Vale, Norman and I walked down the hill and past the historic wooden water tower, which was at one time part of the old Empress jam factory. The tower is quite striking when you see it behind the roadside shrubbery, standing stoically like an old fort or watchtower. The Empress jam "empire" was begun by the pioneer Pease family in the early 1900s. Apparently there was such an abundance of strawberries that the family made jam and canned it in four-pound tins. Their business boomed until an unfortunate mistake led to the demise of the thriving business; they used the wrong kind of sugar for a batch of jam. It was beet sugar, which needed more boiling than regular cane sugar, and the jam fermented in the store and exploded through the tin cans. Well, that's where the sugar mistake occurred, at the water tower!

The Jam Factory

These days, with all our modern health regulations and inspections of food products, fermented jam would not be sold to the public—it is even regulated at roadside stands. But some food products, such as eggs and fruit and vegetables, are still free from government intervention—roadside stands are the last holdout against government inspection. Governmental regulations are at times so ridiculous that it is laughable—I know a butcher who is bald, and the government health inspector made him wear a hairnet!

We cannot leave Cadboro Bay without mentioning a well-loved tree named Jabba the Hut (after the bloated *Star Wars* character). Jabba stands on one of the main boulevards. If a tree has character, this bigleaf maple is a true local personality, a really lovable celebrity! The base of the trunk is extremely thick; it has a very symmetrical bulge, yes, a bulge, like a huge internal swelling of some sort. The limbs stretch from this deformity in a natural way and the dear tree looks healthy and is full of leaves which create a great shady canopy. People have their photos taken sitting amongst the spreading branches. The bulging trunk may be due to one of nature's deformations—it is what's known as a burl, and it is this bulging deformation that gives the lovely tree such a personality. It is not grotesque in any way, but fascinating, voluptuous, and huggable. It's as if the tree is saying, "I'm proud to be a plus size!"

If a person had this deformity, we might very well consider it ugly, strange, and perhaps even a little bit frightening (sometimes there is a very fine line between fascinating and frightening, especially for children). However, when a tree has such a deformity, we often see it differently, as an interesting freak of nature, and perhaps with a little more empathy than we would show an unfortunate person. (Frankly, the wonderful bulging tree reminded me of a gross man I saw one time at an "all you can eat buffet" at a resort in Hawaii. But

with the tree, it isn't self-indulgence; it is nature, so it doesn't repel me.)

Between all these wonderful woodlands, trails, heritage homes, and meadows, there are small pocket parks, lovingly maintained by caring citizens' groups such as Harry and the Weed Whackers. Along the shoreline of Cadboro Bay, slim yellow kayaks glide and bob in and out of the numerous little sandy coves. Telegraph Bay is where, in 1866, the telegraph cable from the United States arrived (by ship from the San Juan Islands) and Victoria could communicate to the world! The first message received by telegraph to the Victoria office (presumably from the shore) was, "Cable all Okay . . . Take a Drink."

It's a little ironic that Cadboro Bay was the site of this great global occasion and yet today, it seems as if it looks at itself from the sea inward, rather than to what lies beyond. This view is much like the way a private eye might view the world, and with that, I tracked down the private investigator whose card I had picked up—she really does crack murder cases!

Burls, Quilts, and Bigleaf Maples

Burls and quilts are deformities that occur in trees, often seen as bulbous protrusions or swellings. Nobody knows for sure, but the causes are most likely stresses, such as pests, fungi, injury, or shock; another cause may be genetic. It was observed that all the maples at a cemetery had burls, but no evidence was conclusive to say that the graves affected those maples in this way; we can only speculate.

A quilted condition is different from a burl in that the deformity consists of large, bubble-like features within the wood. The grain patterns in this wood are exquisite and no two are ever alike. These beautiful patterns can be seen in the bowls, carvings, furniture, and boxes created by wood turners. Musical instruments are often made from trees with the quilted deformity, perhaps because the wood from a quilt contains more air between the fibres. Hardwoods with these unique, swirling and billowing patterns are highly valued and are sold through various companies with informative websites that include some fascinating photographs.

We can imagine nature's spectacular design inside Jabba's massive, bulging trunk, but until this grand icon of Cadboro Bay meets his maker, the pattern remains a secret!

The bigleaf maple is a multi-stemmed tree commonly found in the Victoria region, and its trunk and branches are often covered in thick moss. This tree is often referred to as "the paddle tree" because its wood was used by our First Nations to make paddles for their canoes. The leaves were also rubbed on the faces of teenage boys to restrict the growth of thick whiskers. (I wonder if it works on other parts of our body.)

The Life of a P.I.

We agreed to meet at the little used-book store–café in James Bay. I was there first, looking out for anybody who came in wearing a trench coat belted at the waist and a low, dark, fedora-type hat. Nobody fit the bill— my P.I. was a little lady in a brown woolly coat and big yellow scarf—name of Jones, Leanne Jones.

Jones was her married name, which she kept because the O was useful on her business card (the card I discovered in the dark Russian restaurant) as a logo for a magnifying glass.

Yes, P.I. Jones uses a magnifying glass; other items in her tool kit are a flashlight, notepad, camera, tape recorder, thermos of coffee, and binoculars.

P.I. Jones's special skills are tracing footprints and reading upside down. She knows how to pick a lock but never does anything illegal in her investigations.

Her training was at a religious security school and the courses were based on the Bible.

She investigates murder cases, but is also hired to spy on the movements of suspected spouses.

P.I. Jones says when she gets to a scene, she can "feel" the violence.

Funniest case: She was once asked to follow a bride, every day for a year. "Where is she now?" the new husband would ask every hour. "Going into the washroom at Zellers," might be P.I. Jones's answer. When the man knew for sure, after a year had passed, that his new wife was loyal to him, he asked the P.I. out on a date!

Advice to up-and-coming P.I.s: "Learn to observe. Respect your intuition," which is what I think she has in common with artists.

Painting on Wallace Drive

CHAPTER TEN

The Saanich Peninsula and Sidney

Saanich is a First Nations word meaning "land that is good to be." Other translations are "the fertile land," "land of clay," and "this fair land."

The peninsula has a rich First Nations and agricultural history; when the "white man" bought up the fertile farmlands from the First Nations peoples in the 1800s, many of them established hop farms. Today the peninsula is a neighbourhood of rural properties, large and small farms and wineries, residential pockets, village centres, marinas and beaches, market gardens, roadside stands, and heritage features including historic country churches and pioneer homes.

The many country lanes of the peninsula are lined with hedgerows (which may include the odd old hop!) and the invasive but sweet and succulent blackberries. They are a main attraction for walkers and cyclists to

pick and take home to make jam, jellies, and syrups (syrups are basically jams and jellies that wouldn't set). Mum never used store-bought pectin—she always said that there was natural pectin in the wild apples she picked in the countryside and which are found still today in the hedgerows or at farmers' markets and the little roadside stands that dot the country roads.

An absolutely delicious treat is a blackberry milkshake—just whip milk, vanilla ice cream, and blackberries in a blender for a very special, local, and wild peninsula late-autumn dessert (top with a mint leaf for adults).

Riders stop to pick wild apples for their horses from ancient, gnarled trees that push through the hedgerows' tangle of hawthorn and wild Nootka rose. Because

135

Hops

The hop plant is a tough climbing vine. Its delicate, light green, cone-like flowers are the female part of the plant and are cultivated to flavour beer—they give the beer a tangy taste. Farmers harvested the hops and dried them in oast houses. *Oast* is an old word meaning "kiln."

There are many global varieties of hops, including a British one called Fuggles (doesn't that just sound so English?). Hops also have medicinal properties. They relieve anxiety, for example, and if you put hops in your pillow, it helps cure insomnia.

William Towner, one of the first pioneers on the peninsula, grew hops; his original plant is still growing in a wet, gravelly drainage ditch and climbs a Hydro pole every spring—the locals and heritage preservationists guard and protect this hop and its location!

An oast house is a unique structure; the hops were laid out over several storeys to dry in the warmth from a wood fire below. The distinctive ventilated roofs were cone-shaped. When the hops cooled they were bagged and sent to the local brewery.

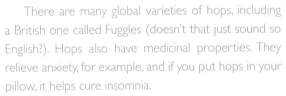

of the peninsula's open green spaces, trail links, hedgerows, beaches, and marine foreshore areas, a vast array of birds and wildlife resides in the country neighbourhood of the Saanich Peninsula.

There's a great difference between the "rural" and "agricultural" properties on the peninsula, but together they create a beautiful countryside within minutes of Victoria. Rural living (which might mean residing on what some urbanites refer to as "martini ranches") means a lifestyle; perhaps the residents have a garden and a lovely marine view, perhaps even some chickens or a horse. Agricultural means *business*!

On the peninsula, there are many agricultural businesses, which include the breeding and selling of special insects intended to eat other insects that attack crops, thereby reducing the need for harmful pesticides. There's a man who grows and sells olive, lemon, and pomegranate trees! There are farms that raise heritage breeds of livestock and poultry such as the Naked Neck hen and the Old Spot pig. And flower growers who make huge, colourful bouquets of dahlias named Yellow Baby, Exotic Dwarf, or Lemon Drop and sell them from great glass jars on the roadside. There are U-pick meadows full of strawberries in June, blueberries in August, and pumpkins and corn in autumn.

St. Stephen's Anglican Church

The peninsula is also home to various wineries, and horse stables, and the oldest church in British Columbia, St. Stephen's. It's a dear little painted structure that sits in a bluebell wood in the heart of the Mount Newton Valley. The lichen-covered, weathered stones in the cemetery wobble like loose teeth under old pear trees and a canopy of huge maples. The odour inside the church is of fresh, damp, cool wood.

Wineries, of course, sell wine, but the vineyard business has also turned into a sort of social and recreational afternoon event. You can taste and sip the local wines while leaning over a smooth,

varnished counter (made from a local tree that was cut down for the vineyard and then reused), and pop little cheese crackers shaped like fish into your mouth while learning how to swirl your glass and how to hold the stem, as well as how to do a sort of gurgle into the wine. This apparently inserts a blast of oxygen, which in turn brings out a multitude of flavours such as "dark cherry," "crisp grapefruit," or "deep vanilla." To me, after a few samples they all taste the same, no matter how I breathe or hold the glass!

Visits to one or two peninsula wineries make for a very pleasant afternoon and you can take a lovely country drive from one to the other (but drive carefully after a tasting!). Many wineries encourage you to stroll through their beautiful landscaped properties, and there's often a lovely old dog to greet you. Winemakers are really out-going, gregarious people. I think the hosting takes up most of their energy—I don't know how they smile all day and pour wine and describe what the heat of your hand does to a merlot or what wine pairs best with a really smelly French cheese. I just couldn't do it!

One winery even started producing gin. The amazing thing about a distillery is the beautiful equipment. Huge, gleaming copper vats with brass fixtures, tubes, and vents, on polished stone floors—distilleries look like the mad scientists' laboratories gone sane.

And then there are the residential areas of the peninsula, usually on slopes for the marine views, with manicured lawns, white front doors, pruned hedges, and mossy baskets of scarlet begonias hanging over freshly painted porches. I heard that in one of these neighbourhoods, a group of residents got together and took a petition to the local council to have their street name changed from Protection Avenue (they thought it sounded too sexual).

By far the biggest and most exciting annual country celebration on the peninsula is the Saanich Fair. It is the oldest continuing fair in western Canada; the first one was held in 1867. At the fair you can see a pig obedience class (it's quite funny!), the tallest sunflower of the year (the record is apparently twenty-five feet), a parade of Arabian horses in native dress, and a three-hundred-pounds-plus pumpkin. You can eat everything from homemade caramel apples to fresh blackberry pie, crispy onion rings from the Lions' caravan to Turkish kabobs. Pioneer farmers demonstrate their antique red and green tractors and steam-powered threshers; prizewinning turkeys strut slowly on their fresh straw, showing off their blue rosettes.

The Saanich Fair is held on Labour Day weekend and marks the end of summer and the beginning of autumn. The dews are heavier, the draft horses' coats are becoming thick, and a fall mist hovers across the fairgrounds at dawn as the

Roadside Stands

The roadside stand just may be the last type of free-market enterprise characterized by two features that symbolize total trust between the seller and the buyer: products on the roadside stand are rarely limited by government regulation, and the money exchange is based on the honour system. The roadside stand typically displays the farmer's wonderful wares—great piles of autumn squash of all shapes, sizes, and colours, free-range eggs from chickens who peck the soil and have dust baths, bouquets of purple kale and burgundy beets, walnuts neatly packaged in cellophane bags, and golden jars of honey from local wildflowers. The buyer is usually instructed, on a colourful painted sign, to deposit the money into a slot.

The income to the farmer often adds up to a nice little sum and as well, any extra produce does not go to waste. The buyers have the satisfaction of knowing where their food came from, as well as the pleasure of shopping *really* locally, and usually just for pocket change. And there's a flood of a good type of feeling at participating in such a trustful relationship; it's like a relief of some sort that trust still exists. That grassroots moment when you drop your coins into the little wooden slot and turn away with your armload of corn is the purest form of honest capitalism.

4-H members, horse grooms, and chicken care-givers clean and feed their livestock before a long day of facing spectators and judges. For three days and nights, the front meadow of the fairgrounds is an array of row upon row of dome tents, tarps, trailers, and mobile homes, and each has a barbecue and a circle of plastic lawn chairs. This is the Saanich Fair neighbourhood!

The sleepy children who must show their sheep and hold their prize rooster up for the judges' inspection later in the day stagger up to the public washrooms in their pyjamas as the dawn creeps over the makeshift village through the mist that has settled overnight. Their mothers make coffee and oatmeal and eggs on the camp stoves in the damp grass as the exhibitors go from the wash-room to the stables, still groggy, emptying the fresh hay and grain into the cages and livestock pens of their charges. This is the part of the fair that the public never sees—they arrive later, bustling through the gates and dashing toward the midway and candy kiosks.

Around noon it can be blazing hot and the judges walk around in their grey smocks pinning great gold and purple rosettes on the winning animals' pens. The exhibitors do not have the fun of heading off to the spinning and tumbling midway; they must remain

with their animals to care for them throughout the day and explain to the fairgoers the business and science required to keep livestock.

I once saw a lovely, gentle farm boy holding his doe-eyed Jersey cow on the end of a rope, stroking her face as she quietly chewed on her hay. He was telling a young family that her name was Dora, and that Jerseys give us the richest milk of any cow breed, and that Dora spends six hours a day eating, and eight hours a day chewing her cud. Dear docile Dora let the children feed her a handful of grain and brush her smooth, fawn-coloured coat. The scene was so refreshing: the nice boy and the little children being so gentle with the cow—it gave me great hope for the world.

One of the more peaceful and rural areas of the peninsula is Ardmore in North Saanich. It has shady, tree-lined lanes connected by pretty trails, and little beaches that look across Saanich Inlet to the layered, deep purple hills of the distant Cowichan Valley. *Ardmore* is an old Scottish word meaning "hard moor."

My friends Lorna and Patrick live in a lovely, airy white house surrounded by a manicured Japanese garden of clipped shrubs, smooth granite boulders, bamboo gates, and a beautiful shallow pond where they used to keep two turtles, named

Continued on page 146

Hedgerows

Among the first peoples to plant hedgerows were the Vikings. When they invaded England, they built strong fences out of dead logs, branches, and sticks to define their boundaries and pen their livestock. It was an arduous process, and one day they realized that if they actually *planted* a live hedgerow, the results would be far more permanent, and far less repair work would be needed every year.

Hedgerows are nature's fences and serve many purposes, especially if they include native plantings. They make good wind and noise buffers and act as pollution absorbers; they prevent erosion and are an excellent source of food, shelter, and habitat for bees, butterflies, birds, and other wildlife. Natural hedgerows can be seen throughout the Saanich Peninsula. North Saanich even has a hedgerow policy, which encourages residents to plant, maintain, and enhance hedgerows, to hand prune, and to resist pruning in the spring when birds nest in the hedgerows. Local nurseries are encouraging residents to landscape with hedgerows and to buy native plants.

Some lovely-sounding native plants that are in our local hedgerows include the Nootka rose, trumpet honeysuckle, snowberry, ocean spray, Indian plum, salmonberry, red flowering currant, beaked hazelnut, and Oregon grape. Doesn't this sound like a delicious hedgerow?!

The Nootka Rose

The word *Nootka* comes from a First Nations word that means "go around." When Captain Cook explored our waters in the 1700s, he named places according to the Native languages. The story is that the local people in Nootka Sound called out, "*Noot'ka*," meaning that he should go around a point, and Cook assumed it was the name of the sound.

The lovely Nootka rose has a delicate, fragrant pink blossom which bees and butterflies love. In the winter, the prickly thickets of the bush are ablaze with crimson and orange rosehips against our low, grey, drizzly skies.

The First Nations used the rose for many ailments and day-to-day needs; the leaves could add flavour to cooked food, tea from the branches soothed the eyes, the chewed leaves eased the stings of bees, and the ripe hips were cooked and mashed and fed to babies with indigestion.

Winemaking and Other Old Trades

My friends Pat and Lamont have a small winery in the heart of the peninsula. There were all sorts of things I wanted to know about our local grape industry, so we had a chat in a lovely loft above the room where the oak barrels are stacked—the barrels are made in British Columbia, by a cooper. Making oak barrels is a very old trade and you could pay a thousand dollars for one from France made from a very specific oak! The type of oak influences the flavour of the wine. The barrels are skilfully constructed and "toasted" on the inside. Originally, coopers made the barrels not only for wine, but also to ship and store gunpowder

and tobacco. The staves are split from the centre of an oak where it is the strongest, shaped with sharp hand tools, then heated and bent into shape to fit snugly; tight iron rings keep the barrel together. Old-fashioned names for these barrels were puncheons, hogsheads, and firkins. French oak barrels are usually used to age the wine because they have a particular flavour; for example, the Limousin oak has a rich vanilla essence that it gives to aging wine.

The big four grapes that can grow on our peninsula are Pinot Noir, Pinot Gris, Marechal Foch, and Ortega. If the soil is too organically rich, the grape will put too much vigour into its leaves and not enough into its grapes. Grapes like the soil to be a little acidic, with good drainage, and they like LOTS of sun and warmth. Growing grapes is a science—the temperature is very closely monitored and recorded, every half-hour in the growing season. Some wineries make fruit wines. The first commercial winery in British Columbia was set up in 1921 and used loganberries. Today, blackberries, picked wild from the sun-drenched summer hedgerows, are a superb winemaking fruit.

Most wine producers do not crush their grapes barefoot anymore (what with our new health regulations and such!). The difference between red and white wine is what happens with the skin; in a white wine, the grapes are pressed first and then the juice ferments; in a red wine, the grapes ferment first, with the seeds and skin still intact, and then they are pressed.

The government has strict health and administrative regulations on winemaking; there is quite a complicated process if a winemaker wishes to sell his or her wines in a liquor outlet, so many peninsula winemakers sell instead from their vineyards. It is far less bureaucratic and much more social and intimate (like a good wine!).

The peninsula attracts many artisans and craftspeople who practise old-fashioned trades; the ironic thing is that these trades today are associated with pleasure and perhaps wealth, while in the past, they were considered quite laborious.

Take the horse farrier. Horse owners prefer to have shoes on their horses to prevent the hooves from wearing too thin and being bruised from riding on hard ground.

To shoe a horse properly, the old trade of blacksmithing, or working with iron, must be employed. Farriers on the peninsula drive to the stables in their trucks, which carry portable forges and very heavy anvils. The farrier has to make the shoe from strips of iron by heating up the metal until it glows red and then pounding it to the shape of the horse's hoof, and every hoof, like our feet, is different. The shoe is nailed onto the hoof red-hot! Neither the nail nor the burning iron hurts the horse because the hoof is like a toenail and has to be cut anyway, and filed down. The art of making *and* fitting horseshoes is an ancient skill and takes years of practice. They say that once horses in ancient times were shod, it changed the course of history—horses in war could run faster and for longer periods without damaging their hooves. (War on horseback changed dramatically again when the Chinese invented the stirrup, which improved the rider's balance enormously.)

The ancient art of boatbuilding is alive and well in the charming village of Brentwood Bay. Brentwood is a sleepy little town overlooking Saanich Inlet. A few years ago it underwent a makeover; flower beds were added down the centre of the street and a roundabout was constructed at the top of the hill, which slowed down the traffic. The south end of Brentwood is dotted with small farms where huge crops of corn and squash are available in the autumn from their market stands. To the west, the neighbourhood of modest houses slopes gently toward the inlet, where one

discovers a quaint historical shoreline area of cozy cafés, kayak rentals, a marina, and a labyrinth of tiny lanes leading to a wood-and-metal building perched on the shore on solid stilts, home to the boatbuilders and restorers Abernethy and Gaudin. Boat repair makes these men their money, but their passion, and what they also practise for love, is actual old-fashioned boatbuilding.

Hanging from the high-beamed, dust-covered ceiling were a few of their works of art: a pea pod-shaped rowboat, a replica of a little wooden boat that was used to fish salmon in the inlet in the 1940s; a Newfoundland dory; and a beautiful, elegant boat that was used on the St. Lawrence River. "The white man's canoe," said an apprentice in worn canvas overalls as he looked up from sanding, by hand, a pair of wooden oars.

A freshly varnished mast with polished brass hooks and rings lay ready to be stepped in a little sailboat bobbing at the wharf, just a few yards away outside in the sunlight. I realized that you could actually tell the history of Canada by its variety of little wooden boats. The red cedar and oak in the canoe was hand steamed (just as at the cooperage) and then copper riveted.

Saanich Inlet has a long history of industry, and evidence still can be seen—the old limestone quarry at The Butchart Gardens, the remnants of the brick factory all through the woods and trails at nearby Tod Inlet, and the crumbling old grey cement plant across the inlet, now overgrown with natural bushes, blackberries, and climbing vines.

The boatbuilders offered to introduce me to a man who knows much of the inlet's fishing history—"an old salty guy," they said—but he was nowhere to be found on the day I visited. There's something romantic about being an old salty guy, of having a life on the sea; that's part of the appeal of old crafts and skills such as boatbuilding. Being in the present, but working with the past, working with the memories that have brought us where we are, keeps that connection to what formed us.

But I do wonder whether in another eighty years, when boatbuilders are restoring the great white fibreglass yachts of today, it will feel *as* romantic, working with chrome and resin rather than with wood and brass. I wonder if it is simply the past that is romantic, or if it is truly the traditions, the materials, the morals, and the feelings of society rather than just the passing of time.

Brentwood Bay Shipyard

Continued from page 140

Blanche and Sparky. Blanche and Sparky often sunned themselves on the lily pads or the granite patio alongside us as we drank our gin and tonics during the warm summer, but one day Blanche disappeared. Lorna was so upset that she posted a LOST sign, offering a reward, on the corner Hydro pole, and the only person who answered her was an animal psychic; she said that Blanche was "still on the earth and was at peace in the universe," and that for one hundred dollars she might be able to locate her. I think (from reading about turtle behaviour) that Blanche lumbered off to the creek across the road to mate and lay her eggs along the clay banks under the great drooping cedars. That's what turtles do. Poor Lorna grieved for days. Blanche never showed up again.

Victoria International Airport

The Victoria International Airport covers a lot of area, as you can imagine, but the forward-thinking managers and board have created an airport that is part farm, part heritage, part business, part park, and part protected ecosystem. And most of these features are open to the public to enjoy. Gentle, cud-chewing Holsteins lie in the airport meadows, and in mid-summer the meadows are hayed by a local farmer. The new campus-style business buildings on part of the airport land are not only low (good thing!) but attractive and blend into the landscape. There is a lovely, safe, wide bicycle path around most of the airport and plans to complete the perimeter; on the south side is a little forest and a creek and a glade of trees, which are protected for the skylarks to nest in, and on the north side is a rolling meadow with our native Garry oak trees, which the airport has acknowledged as being a heritage site—the site of a wartime hospital.

Public art is a main feature of the airport, both inside and out. We are greeted in the parking lot by huge, nodding, colourful flowers in front of the turquoise glass entrance, to say hello and goodbye to all travellers. What a wonderful last image to leave Victoria by, and such a glorious welcome home! This is the great significance of these joyous flowers.

The first pilot to land on the runway at the airport was George DuTemple. His son, Wally, owns the Ardmore Golf Course. Wally keeps a "green" golf course—it used to be his family's farm, and Wally still allows his donkeys to roam the greens amongst the old apple trees and hedgerows of hawthorns.

Sidney-by-the-Sea

On the east side of the peninsula is the little seaside hub of Sidney. The carved blue welcoming sign sits on Beacon Avenue at the highway, and invites

you to explore this delightful and unique town. In recent years, Sidney has beautified every street leading to its centre; there are lifelike bronze statues created by sculptor Nathan Scott sitting on the public benches all the way along Beacon Avenue. Every time I come out of Tanner's Books I get a start, seeing the old bronze lady reading on the corner! And there's an old man on a bench down near the wharf, sitting and reflecting with his hands folded in his lap, and every day somebody places a small bouquet of fresh flowers in his fingers.

This is what makes Sidney very special—the people (visitors and residents) involve themselves with the feeling and features of the town. They actually feel part of the community—they really *do* ask themselves what they can do to help and enhance the town, rather than ask what the town can do for them.

There are flower tubs everywhere and mini-gardens on the boulevards brimming with lush colour, and a quaint little museum in the old post office. The museum has exhibits ranging from the history of tea to teddy bears to quilts to Lego creations.

Down at the end of Beacon Avenue is the wharf where, in the summer, you can take a little boat ride to nearby Sidney Spit, a long and elegant arc of white sand that gently curves into the sea. There's a traditional fish market on the wharf too, in a rustic building made of blue corrugated tin with yellow trim, with local art displayed on the sides.

There are also more than a few consignment and secondhand stores, which are great fun. There is even a "thrift shop" that has rescued cats up for adoption—they stretch out amongst the plastic flowers and chipped china, faded men's ties, water-stained vases, tarnished candlesticks, and musty-smelling green drapes. They hide between the boxes of donated clothing and behind tired-looking furniture, or sit and glare at you from the shelves of yellowed how-to books.

A tourist magazine said that Sidney

attracts mid-life retirees, but that didn't stop Sidney-by-the-Sea from once having a "love shop"—it was over the vacuum store. There is a quaint and charming cinema with worn red seats that shows opera and interesting documentaries (along with popular features), and before each film is shown, the owner strolls down the aisle and welcomes you to the cinema and tells you a little about the production. Every so often the poor owner stands wringing her hands and explains that the projector has broken down or overheated and you are given a rain check, but that is all part of the charm and you just head for an espresso instead, and take an evening stroll along the wharves and piers, under the stars.

Sidney also loves its local culture. The well-known Canadian poet Al Purdy lived nearby and after he died, a group of intelligent, cultured people honoured Al by wrapping his words around a Hydro box in front of the bank!

Sidney seems to have everything. There is a spacious marina full of polished white yachts and sailboats with lovely fresh names such as *Wind Walker* or *Moon Prancer* painted on them in elegant blue letters, a sea walk and a little band shelter for summer concerts. There's a bakery, an ice cream parlour, a library, a rose garden, and a long, clean, beautiful pebble beach. You can rent kayaks and glide along the quiet, shallow shoreline, over the kelp beds and between little islets, around the bays and alongside the wharves lined with luxurious flower baskets of pink petunias and blue lobelia. There used to be two swans that loved to paddle beside the kayaks, and every year they had a little flock of grey fuzzy babies who would come along too.

Sidney, like many small towns, never used to be so charming, quaint, and physically attractive, but in the last ten years, there has been a "small town rejuvenation" and recognition of the importance of art, architectural design, aesthetic pleasure, beauty, intelligence, and a certain kind of cultural ease. Because of these improvements, better, healthier businesses have arrived or been enhanced—imagination and the idea of being "different" in Sidney are now embraced after a long period in our society when simply making money from business was the only goal. Architecture was dull, as stucco boxes went up everywhere (and often they leaked and were mildewed); taste and design weren't even thought about and humour was absent—it would be a serious thing, for example, for a movie projector to break down, but now people love the idea of a homegrown little cinema business and accept the reality of small-business problems, which can and do arise, with much more compassion and empathy. The world is in a better place, much as it is difficult to see sometimes, but a small seaside town such as Sidney is living proof—there is indeed more of a feeling for beauty, humour, compassion and a thirst for a better society all around us. If you think about it, these four driving forces—beauty, humour, compassion, and desire for goodness—are related, and they work together.

One of the unique features of Sidney is that it is a "book town." Sidney has had as many as

ten bookshops at one time, operating within a few blocks of each other—one summer there were *sixteen* bookshops! There are used-book stores (some with priceless and rare literary treasures), bookstores selling only paperbacks, a military bookshop, and bookshops selling books on country crafts. Being a book town is yet another wonderful, fun, and intelligent branding of this lovely town. I love the fact that they are supporting books—how courageous and original in a world that seems to enjoy looking at screens more than turning pages. Book towns such as Sidney also host literary festivals and many arts events—the venues are in coffee shops, parks, and even in the Ocean Discovery Centre. I once did a book reading there in front of a tank full of huge, curious, and attentive fish.

There are many official book towns in the world, including Tokyo and, if you can believe it, a place called Archer City in Texas! The enterprise of bookbinding is also going on in Sidney. The craft required to design and bind beautiful books dates from the medieval ages when monks spent hours alone in their cells creating their illuminated manuscripts. The dedicated and patient bookbinders hand sew, not glue, the pages to the spine, and often include headbands, elaborately decorated trims and front pages, gilt fore edges, and silk ribbons that serve as bookmarks. Binding can be made from leather or cloth.

Some booklovers not only lovingly bind books, but print them too, on antique printing presses. My friends who work in one of the many Sidney bookstores have a cast-iron, 1900 Chandler and Price printing press in their basement and every so often undertake the grand project of printing a book; they use handmade paper and they have to do one page at a time before resetting the letters. Their books, cards, and leaflets are beautiful labours of love and works of art, often with engravings or woodcuts as illustrations; the work is not mass produced but is created as limited editions.

The Globe and Mail had a very stimulating article on the importance of the printed book. It referred to printed books as "artifacts of the human mind"—the books are passed down and studied as "print culture." Margin notes can reveal all sorts of thoughts, and the material or type of leather binding can distinguish the wealth and location of the publisher. Perhaps the most interesting and relevant quote in Ian Brown's article was from Professor Elizabeth Harvey; she said that "books were made to be touched." Paper and leather and the oils from the inks give the reader a very close physical connection with the book; she also said that reading a physical book is like "visiting a historic site." I love her perspective and I think so do many others who shop in Sidney, the book town, for the great art of the book!

Of course the peninsula, being a peninsula, also has lovely beaches. One of the most delightful is Island View Beach, in the heart of the agricultural belt in Central Saanich. You drive down a country lane to the beach and pass a long stretch of rolling, fertile fields full of cabbages, little flower stands, a strawberry kiosk, and a goat farm, and then you come upon the wonderful wild view of the sea and the windswept, sandy cliffs of the islands just off the shore.

The two main features of Island View Beach are its amazing, endless silver sand strips, exposed at low tide, and its rather rustic carved trail along the shore atop a berm. On the seaward side of the berm is a unique salt-washed landscape that begins as a grassy meadow, then turns into a dark amber peat bog, and finally, at the end of the trail, becomes a meadow of sand dunes and sun-washed, sea-bleached grasses and stunted sedums. These dunes are little ecosystems where specific rare flora can grow, and these specialized, salt-air plants host numerous endangered species, both plant and animal.

In this particular sand-dune ecosystem grows a rare little grassy plant called the yellow sand verbena. It has a delicate trumpet flower and is the host plant to a very rare, tiny moth called the sand verbena moth. The moth is very vulnerable because it depends *only* on this specific plant to feed and breed, so projects are constantly under way to maintain and enhance the sand-dune eco-system—the sand verbena moth is only found in ten locations in the world!

The stark and barren sand-dune area at the end of Island View Beach is a transition zone between the sea and an inland mass of lush shrubbery and a marshy meadow where many seabirds nest. Natural landscape transitions are fascinating and house a multitude of diverse plant and animal life only feet

Restoring a stream and watercourse requires a few special procedures. The first thing the volunteers do is clean out the litter. Tests are done to determine water quality, then the real work begins. Water flow must be *increased*, usually from a source upstream. Riffles, which are rows of small boulders across the streambed, are built to create oxygen as the flow rushes over the ledge. In some cases the streambed may have to be restored with gravel, or reshaped by redirecting the water.

The Restoration of the Peninsula's Streams

Between the farms and residential neighbourhoods, market gardens, wineries, and horse stables, the peninsula is a maze of watersheds, lakes, grasslands, and salmon streams. The areas along these watercourses are called riparian. There is a current environmental movement to restore the streams, watersheds, and riparian areas on the peninsula—not only to enhance them, but to encourage salmon spawning. On weekends you may spot a group of dedicated volunteers in bright yellow, muddied rain gear and rubber boots, busily working in and around streambeds and on misty fields, often in the dismal, raw winter rains, bringing the life force back to a stagnant or polluted pond.

But one of the most important processes is to restore the natural environment on the streambanks; this involves removing invasive plants such as English ivy and Scotch broom, which choke out native plants, and replanting with beneficial species such as red alder and willow, which prevent erosion and stabilize the banks. The plants also provide shade to cool the stream in hot weather, and give natural wildlife a habitat and marsh birds a nesting site. Finally, salmon eggs are deposited in the stream. Other stream life will soon appear as the stream returns to a healthy, living, breathing ecosystem.

apart. Sometimes I wish that humans could handle transitions as well as nature.

On a blustery summer day, the sea at Island View Beach is full of the colourful sails of wind-surfers. The paragliders are attached by long, thick lines to slim and flexible figures in rubber wetsuits, knees bent and leaning against the winds and waves, always hoping for, always anticipating, that surge and moment of perfection (as an artist does) when they will be carried into the air or sea on that ideal angle that nature has spontaneously thrown at them. Perhaps what they are striving for is to be at one with nature, if only for a moment.

Elk and Beaver Lakes—A Natural Neighbourhood

The largest public freshwater area on the peninsula is Elk and Beaver Lakes (they are joined). These lovely lakes are surrounded by a six-mile trail where many recreational activities are enjoyed. You can stroll through the woods and listen to the lake lapping along its rocky shore as you see horseback riders, dog walkers, and, in some areas, recreational cyclists. There are picnic areas under the willow trees and several safe, sandy swimming beaches.

Rowers, kayakers, and canoeists use the lake, as do, in specified areas, motorboats. On a breezy, sunny day you can see people fishing from the shore or from little rubber dinghies, or our Olympic rowing team practising, led by a little yelling man with a megaphone, or a water skier, or a canoe full of birdwatchers sitting quietly in the reeds.

The landscape is a diverse combination of forest, grassland, and wetland, and is home to many species of native flora and fauna—the lake, however, is threatened by the invasive giant American bullfrog, which can consume a small duckling. These bullfrogs are being dealt with by our busy Parks workers, to help preserve the lake's natural ecosystem. The giant bullfrog was originally bred in New England for its legs, a delicious delicacy. Over time, the frog, like all great explorers, made its way west.

Although Elk and Beaver Lakes are not neighbourhoods per se, they are indeed *natural* neighbourhoods with freshwater life cycles, food chains, and thriving ecosystems. Along the walk are

pillows and is gathered by marsh birds to line their cozy nests; the cattail is also a delicious vegetable—the peeled shoot makes a lovely cucumber type of crunchy salad enhancer; and the golden pollen is highly nutritious and can also be made into a flour.

And there's more! The jelly substance between the leaves soothes wounds and boils and carbuncles. Nobody speaks of carbuncles these days—it's an old condition rarely seen, just like quinsy and consumption and chilblains. Carbuncles are similar to a boil, but worse. The word sounds rather English, like something Gran would have suffered with in a damp English cottage on a bleak moor in winter.

And if these uses of the fabulous cattail aren't enough, here are even more. The dried seed heads light easily and the smoke will repel annoying insects; the cattails also absorb water pollution from their lake, marsh, or ditch, and purify the water. According to the "wild man," Steve Brill, who has a wonderful website on this amazing plant, cattails have been planted along the Nile River to reduce salinity.

several areas of marsh full of bulrushes. The bulrush, or cattail, is often referred to as "the shopping centre of the pond" because it has so many uses. The leaves can be woven into baskets, furniture, hats, and mats (the little wren uses the leaves to weave his multitude of lovely homes to attract a wife) and can even thatch a roof; the cattail fluff from the seed can be used as warm stuffing for

A marsh thick with bulrushes and cattails is also home to the stunning red-winged blackbird, who wears the classiest and most tasteful outfit of all birds in my opinion—he is slim and black and elegant, with just a dash of red and gold on his shoulder. The blackbird nests in little woven cups sealed with clay amongst the stately, modest bulrushes.

A silent creature who quietly resides in Elk and Beaver Lakes is our endangered western painted turtle (the only native freshwater turtle in British Columbia). This little animal has a beautiful, colourful pattern on its underside (the plastron) and loves to crawl up the muddy banks of the lakes and make its way to secluded sandy spots on the edge of the forests to breed. Environmental groups are protecting the turtles' nesting sites. The turtles can be seen on the lakes from a quiet canoe, often sunning themselves on logs or stones or on the warm muddy shore; they bask in the heat to dry their shells and rid themselves of algae. They feed in the morning and bask in the afternoon, the way people do in Spain! Turtles have no teeth but eat with their sharp, shapely beaks.

When a male turtle is attracted to a female, he entices her by stroking

Scotch Broom

We have all seen this beautiful and invasive, brilliant yellow flowering shrub thriving in the hardest, most unfertile soils, even in rock crevices. (Its cousin is the thorny gorse, which covers the cliffs of Dallas Road and seems to love the salt gales that blow it hard against the clay bluffs. Gorse may be invasive, but it's keeping the seaside cliffs intact—sometimes invasive and tough can be a good thing. Trust the Scots!).

Broom most likely received its name because it was bunched together and used as a broom way back in Anglo-Saxon times—*brom* meant "foliage" and *besoms* meant "broom." The Latin name for Scotch broom is *Planta genista*; the early medieval British king Geoffrey V chose the sprig of broom as his badge, and thereafter the British dynasty was named the Plantagenets. The Plantagenets ruled England from 1154 to 1485. Imagine this great virile dynasty being named after a little yellow flower! Well, come to think of it, the broom plant is pretty tough, tough but pretty—like the kings of that time!

and tickling her head for fifteen minutes! (Oh, there's nothing like a head massage—it's heaven. When someone massages my head, I succumb to a lovely trance, but unlike the turtle, it has nothing to do with sex.) When the female turtle is ready to lay her eggs, she chooses a place that is warm, faces south, and is easy digging. The temperature of the eggs determines the gender of the babies. If the nest is cooler, there will be more males hatched.

Researching a little bit about turtles on a drizzly, raw winter's afternoon, I found some very interesting facts. There are three hundred species of turtles on the planet; forty-four live in Canada, and four are native to British Columbia—our western painted turtle, the western pond turtle, the green sea turtle, and the leatherback. The sea turtles eat jellyfish, which is why I pick up trash on the beaches—sea turtles mistake plastic for jellyfish and choke on it.

An article in our local paper reported on a species of turtle never before seen in our local waters, the Olive Ridley turtle. It's a warm-water sea turtle, so why is it here? They nest on the Californian and Mexican coasts and are considered threatened in the United States. The difference between a tortoise and a turtle is that tortoises are terrestrial and have a heavier shell.

Eighty-four percent of the fish in Elk and Beaver Lakes are the pumpkinseed sunfish; although it has a pretty name (I have visions of a golden, elegant fish gliding amongst the pond grasses), this sunfish is an introduced species. One native fish in the lake is the prickly sculpin, with not such a pretty name! The lake is stocked annually with our native rainbow trout (another pretty name), which attract the fishermen.

On the south side of the lake, the path winds its way under willow trees and past pocket beaches and meadows of wildflowers. It is worth a short stop at the Nature House, a little brick nook tucked amongst the woods, just down from the parking lot. The Nature House contains displays on everything from the various types of bird nests to posters describing what a group of jellyfish is called—a smack! (Other groups of animals are thus: a murder of crows, a charm of finches, a prickle of porcupines, a parliament of owls, and a knot of toads.) Those would be quite the neighbourhoods!

This seems a fitting end to our neighbourhood observations, with the place where so many residents congregate to admire Victoria's beauty: to stroll and stop for a salal berry on the lakeshore; to drift in a little rowboat in the lily pads with a fishing line; to watch the birds going about their daily activities in the reeds; to walk in the forest with a loyal dog companion, or to sit amongst the wildflowers with the sun's heat on your back and have a little think, because you never know what discovery or thought may come upon you at any moment. A thought or discovery might change your life, or simply give you a moment's joy, whether it be seeing the winter return of the little harlequin duck bobbing on a misty green sea-storm day, or puzzling over a piece of public art gleaming in the sun, or wondering if Captain Cook really did have such lovely legs as he stands over Victoria and its neighbourhoods.

The History of Elk and Beaver Lakes

The land around these lakes, like most other parts of the region, was home for thousands of years to First Nations. But when Victoria was establishing itself and spreading out toward the peninsula, it needed much of the resources, such as freshwater, and in the 1850s, the City purchased the entire peninsula for 386 wool blankets.

At this time, Elk and Beaver Lakes were separate, but they became one when engineers dammed nearby Colquitz Creek. The water was pumped into town, but the residents complained of tadpoles in their drinking water! So filter beds were built at the lake. The lake was also used for skating and swimming; in the 1930s and '40s, there was a popular tea house, an outdoor dance hall, and a chocolate factory! (Victoria's water source at present is the Sooke Reservoir).

Index

Acknowledgments

I'd like to thank my publisher, Ruth Linka, and editor, Marlyn Horsdal, for once again offering me the opportunity to write and publish my words and thoughts, and the helpful, professional staff at TouchWood Editions.

Artist and friend Robert Amos deserves a special thank-you for keeping my nose to the grindstone, providing constant words of encouragement and enthusiasm, and for our ventures out and about exploring our neighbourhoods but "never going too far away" and for recognizing the differences in the way we see things.

Thanks to Sarah Amos for providing a few of the paintings: duck, page 23; camas, page 52; both birds, page 128; swallow, page 129; turtle, page 154.

Thanks to Mikki Richards for dealing with the maddening and frustrating computer technology and technical editing, and putting up with me when I screamed in panic and thought my life was over when the screen went blue.

And thank you to those who so generously and willingly gave up their time to tell me their memories and stories, show me their neighbourhoods, and share their thoughts: Norman Morgenstern, Elizabeth Borek, Leanne Jones, Pat George and Lamont Brooks of Symphony Winery, Bill Dancer, compost and permaculture experts Marika Smith and volunteer Sandy, Heather Chatwin, Jane Henderson, Sister Frieda Raab, Joan Byers, Elizabeth Levinson, Clayton Jevne, Jean Gaudin, and Ashley Bleims.

And thank you to Joan and Hazel for the good feedback on our beach walks.

Thank you all for making Victoria's neighbourhoods so beautiful, so kind, and so cultured.